THE FINALITY OF FAITH

other books by NELS F. S. FERRÉ

SWEDISH CONTRIBUTIONS TO MODERN THEOLOGY
THE CHRISTIAN FELLOWSHIP
THE CHRISTIAN FAITH
RETURN TO CHRISTIANITY
FAITH AND REASON
EVIL AND THE CHRISTIAN FAITH
PILLARS OF FAITH
CHRISTIANITY AND SOCIETY
THE CHRISTIAN UNDERSTANDING OF GOD
STRENGTHENING THE SPIRITUAL LIFE
THE SUN AND THE UMBRELLA
CHRISTIAN FAITH AND HIGHER EDUCATION
MAKING RELIGION REAL
CHRIST AND THE CHRISTIAN
KNOW YOUR FAITH
SEARCHLIGHTS ON CONTEMPORARY THEOLOGY
GOD'S NEW AGE

The Finality of Faith

AND

CHRISTIANITY AMONG

THE WORLD RELIGIONS

By NELS F. S. FERRÉ

ABBOT PROFESSOR OF CHRISTIAN THEOLOGY

ANDOVER NEWTON THEOLOGICAL SCHOOL

GREENWOOD PRESS, PUBLISHERS
WESTPORT, CONNECTICUT

Library of Congress Cataloging in Publication Data

Ferré, Nels Fredrick Solomon, 1908-
    The finality of faith and Christianity among
the world religions.

        Reprint of the ed. published by Harper & Row,
New York.
        1.   Faith.   2.   Christianity and other religions.
I.   Ferré, Nels Fredrick Solomon, 1908-
Christianity among the world religions.   1979.
II.   Title: The finality of faith.
[BT771.2.F4   1979]   234'.2   78-11979
    ISBN 0-313-21182-5

Grateful acknowledgment is made to the publishers of the following periodicals for permission to reprint, in revised form, the articles indicated:

UNITED CHURCH HERALD for "Is the Basis of the World Council Heretical?" May 17, 1962 (Chapter 7: "Reflections on the Basis of the World Council of Churches"); "Are Missions Worth Saving?" October 18, 1962 (Chapter 8: "Redefining the Task of Christian Missions"). THE CHRISTIAN CENTURY for "A Theology for Missions," November 21, 1962 (Chapter 6, "The Universal Dimensions of the Christian Faith").
THE PULPIT for "Christianity Among the World Religions," September, 1961 (Chapter 5: "Christianity and World Faith").

Reprinted with the permission of Harper & Row, Publishers, Inc.

Reprinted in 1979 by Greenwood Press, Inc.,
51 Riverside Avenue, Westport, CT 06880

Printed in the United States of America

10 9 8 7 6 5 4 3 2 1

To
Herbert Gezork
colleague and friend

Contents

Preface

Once again a book! But this one is different. Many will charge that I have changed. And so I have! Perhaps a year's trip around the world, with many and long discussions with non-Christian thinkers, scholars and ordinary people alike, has made the difference. All I know is that a new feeling has come over me. I have both suffered much and found fresh sources of satisfaction in this new climate. My faithful readers, for whom I am ever grateful, can share this experience to some extent with me and judge for themselves.

Never have I understood as now the need for faith. My experience keeps humbling me increasingly into such an appreciation.

The immediate occasion for the writing of this volume was the preparation for the Otts Lectures at Davidson College in North Carolina. My thanks go to President D. Grier Martin, the faculty, and the students.

The second section of the book was written concurrently with the Otts Lectures in connection with the world trip, in the course of which I discussed the basic questions of the

relation of the Christian faith to the major non-Christian
religions with both Christian missionary leaders and non-
Christian thinkers of high integrity and exceptional
competence. Mahayana Buddhist and Shinto scholars in
Japan, Chinese Confucian and Taoist thinkers, Theravada
Buddhists in Burma, sages of several kinds of Hinduism in
India, both officials and laymen, and Muslim legal minds
and students in the Near East have made me probe deeply
into my own faith. During the year, too, I kept reading and
pondering both non-Christian literature and Christian writ-
ings concerning other fields. I can never be the same! With
the impressions still pulsingly fresh I wrote four papers for
immediate publication that have concrete bearing on the
main issues of the book. The chapter on the basis of the
World Council I consider especially important in its direct
bearing on our relating ourselves honestly and effectively to
the non-Christian religions.

I am thankful to the *United Church Herald, The Christian
Century,* and *The Pulpit* for permission to use these.

Once again thanks to the Religious Books Department of
Harper & Row for their unfailing and exemplary support, to
Mrs. Robert Suddath for typing the final manuscript, and to
my wife who as usual typed more than one draft as well as
offered suggestions for improvement. My final thanks are to
God, for I have never been more conscious of the constant
grace I receive.

NELS F. S. FERRÉ

September, 1962
Newton Centre, Massachusetts

PART I

THE FINALITY
OF FAITH

1: The Focus of Faith

To have finality of faith does not mean having the final answers. Whoever knows all the answers has no faith. What he has is knowledge. The finality of faith, on the contrary, involves *not* knowing final answers. The finality of faith expresses the truth precisely that faith is final, not as knowledge but as faith on the move toward finding.

As finite human beings we have no choice but faith. We cannot know as God knows. If at the end our destiny is to "know as we are known," such finality does not belong to human history. As finite beings we are forced to have faith, and never to go beyond it. Therefore faith is both our problem and our potential. Our problem is that we cannot escape faith. Our faith is as much forced as is our freedom. Both meaningfulness and meaninglessness are faith judgments; and in between, every human response involves some kind of faith.

[3

Whatever potential life may have is therefore also dependent upon some form of faith.

Some lives show the power of their faith. But then what is the secret of such faith? If the final answers escape us, can we know faith? If we cannot know the destiny, how can we know the direction? How can we know what truth faith is, in other words, if we cannot know the final answers? The fact is, of course, that we cannot know faith any better than its conclusions. Faith must be believed. We must live faith beyond knowledge.

Faith is not knowledge. Perhaps, then, religions have contributed immeasurably to the present failure of faith by offering sight instead of faith. Our approach in this chapter is first to consider the failure of faith, then to see how the fixation of false faith has stood in the way of true faith, and finally to examine the flexible nature of true faith. Our aim, in short, is to find the focus of faith that is never wholly given nor beyond finding.

I

To speak of today's failure of faith is dangerous. Speakers and writers usually do so, for effect. But there never was a day when there was no failure of faith. All of us have had the experience of reading what seems a sharp, precise condemnation of our present generation only to find that the utterance came from, say, Benjamin Franklin. Not long ago I read an indictment of our age that was so completely up to date, that hit the nail so squarely on the head, that I marveled at the writer's skill in articulating our exact feelings.

What a shock to learn that the author had penned those words during the heyday of ancient Greece! Hence we had better not moan over our lost and lone generation as if it were unique. As a matter of fact, a strong case could be made for the proposition that our generation is paying peculiarly intense attention to religion.

All the same, this attention is on the negative side. Although, in general, the intellectuals have seldom been the carriers of positive faith, today's fashion is perhaps peculiarly unbelief. Modern man not only glories but grovels in despair. Nihilism is the style. All of a sudden the happy ending is taboo throughout the whole world of literature.

Even the word "entertainment" has changed its meaning. I learned this one Saturday evening as my daughter fretted around the living room waiting for her date to arrive.

"Last week," she groaned, "he took me to *Waiting for Godot*. Godot never came. The week before we saw a movie, *Hiroshima, Mon Amour*. It was so depressing that neither of us could speak a word the whole way home. Last night we went to a Harvard production of a Tennessee Williams play with a terribly sad story. Daddy, I can hardly bear to go out tonight."

When I suggested that they look for a good healthy comedy somewhere, she wailed in protest,

"Heavens, no! Anything that is worth seeing nowadays is bound to be depressing."

Not morality but meaninglessness dominates the inner standard of the artistic world. Year after year I attend the Boston Arts Festival and notice by the pictures chosen for exhibit and by those awarded prizes how the public taste is gradually being educated to the abstract. Even schoolboys use the word "negoism" for our mood of denial. While, to be sure, no robe of public appearance is seamless, today it is mostly shapeless!

In religion, too, there is a fad, if not yet a full-scale fashion, to announce the death of the gods. The post-Christian era is upon us. Modern man, we hear, has once for all outgrown Christian ideology. Our scientific, historic, social science world view pronounces the Christian faith to be outdated. Some religious writers have tried to take refuge in myths and symbols. The historic faith may be gone, they say; we may not be able to know anything about the ultimate, but we can direct and bolster life by meaningful myths and symbols. But such faith is itself under attack by the post-moderns, who insist that we face the fact that life is meaningless in itself, that reality cannot be known, and that we must adjust ourselves to ultimate despair.

A generation ago Europe led the way into the honesty of meaninglessness. The mood there now seems less sure of nihilism. But today a strong American leadership is ushering us into the dreads or fascinations of the void. It is easy to say that this spiritual "tempeffect" is confined to the intellectual smart set, but the fact is that it is pervading the general background of our age. It is a subtle, intangible mood that seems more to evoke its spokesmen than to be created by them. Current verbalization to be correct must conform to this enveloping drift of opinion.

Both the advocates of myths and symbols and their attackers, however, are basically fighting faith. The former use their tools to escape traditional Christianity; the latter battle to destroy their halting allegiance to the barer truth. For the postmoderns there is no room for faith in science, education, or legislation, except as humanly necessary activities of realistic adjustments to the actual world. These afford no ground for faith. All roads to objectively ascertainable meaning are closed.

In the past it has been common to point to the self-sufficient secularist or to the new Marxist man as proof that there is no need for faith. These people who live as well as the next seemingly get along well without any faith. With a deeper understanding of faith as the total response of life that cannot be proved, however, these secularists and Marxists, even though they may not have a religion, do have faith. But if anything colors our age it is surely the way the erstwhile complacent secularist shares our common anxiety. He now appears far less certain than heretofore of his faith in the need for no religion. The secularists have been streaming back to our churches. As for the Communists, I do not know what is going on among them, but after decades of persecution as well as constant education for godlessness, it appears that the need for faith keeps creating church response even in Russia, and there are repeated reports to the effect that the young Communists are now seeking faith beyond the prescribed ideology of Marxism. Thus there seems to be failure of faith even on the part of the secularists and the Marxists.

From a year's living among the religions of the world, and from conversations with non-Christians, both faculty and students, I learned how the modern mood of negativism toward established religions has eaten deep into the fabric of their consciousness as well. Perhaps it is too much to believe that the collapse of the world religions is imminent. Nevertheless it is true that the same confusion, revolt, and reaching out for something new that we observe in Christianity is an inner part of the experience of non-Christian faiths as well. Buddhism may seem romantic to us as an escape from Christianity, but those long within the faith seem to share our common sufferings over the repudiation of the religions. The Muslim youth may seem safe within the shelter of their infallible Book, beyond the disputations of theology, but intimate conversations with them makes it hard to differentiate them and their problems from Christian students and theirs.

The summary of this survey could perhaps be to the effect that there is less failure of faith than failure of the faiths. Or perhaps we can dare conclude that there may be more seeking for faith in our unprecedented day of danger and of change, while also less definiteness as any content for faith that can satisfy. All faiths are put in question by numberless adherents within them, informal as well as formal faiths, yes, even the faiths that major in the proclamation of unfaith. Men reject the conclusions of faith. They repudiate the answers of faith.

Obviously there are still countless precritical and uncritical believers of every persuasion. Beside them stand an unnumbered multitude who simply do not know whether they believe or not, or how much, or who believe vaguely but do not know what they really believe. These, too, are found within every persuasion. But among the leaders of thought there is definitely a strong movement away from traditional faiths, and within this movement and seemingly often in its lead, are drives and drifts to nihilism, to meaninglessness, and to both a genuine and a fashionable despair. Perhaps this situation is exceptionally healthy. Perhaps there never was an age more ready for faith. Perhaps the greatest obstacle to faith has been the faiths themselves. If the religions have had not faith, but a false faith that denies and destroys true faith, the destruction of these religions may itself be a necessary prelude to faith. Perhaps the protesters of knowledge in the name of myths and symbols, like Bultmann and Tillich, and even the purveyors of so-called unfaith, like Bertrand Russell and Camus, are our strongest allies in the establishment of an age of genuine and creative faith. Let us examine this thesis.

II

The presupposition of our analysis is that faith is movement in the direction of a goal. The goal is not yet seen and the direction is never fully charted. Insofar as direction implies a definite goal, that goal is nevertheless not the kind that can be static or fixed. It is rather "invitation to pilgrimage." It is an offer to try a kind of life that no one can ever live for anyone else. What this means will naturally constitute the heart of our communication, but our task now is to see how false faiths have undermined faith itself. By "faith," in our analysis, I do not mean belief in Christian doctrines. When the specifically Christian faith is intended, I shall use the word "Christian" to make the meaning clear. Religions, instead of being open to dynamic movement, tend to develop fixations of faith. That faith have direction and flow is good, for when religion stagnates faith becomes murky. That faith have enough knowledge to know where to move is a true need; but faith's claim to see the ultimate answers at any present moment dooms it to fixation.

Islam, for example, is peculiarly dogged by its complete identification with the infallible Book. Every Muslim, to be orthodox, must believe that the Koran is infallibly inspired. There were times in the history of Islam when its scholars could have been allowed to become self-critical of its authority, but since al-Ghazzali, Islam has become disastrously yoked with the doctrine of infallibility. Faith, then, becomes acceptance of historic facts and not the continual unfolding of the hazards as well as the wonders of the way.

But our Christian faith also has its own kinds of fixations. Even so, fundamentalism is centrally less a faith than the fighting of faith. Fundamentalism claims to possess in human history infallible truth: an inerrant Bible providing all the answers we need. It craves to live by sight and not by faith. Its quality of absoluteness is commendable; true religion always possesses it. But the absoluteness of fundamentalism is men's possessing the answers in this world. As such it is a Jehovah complex, the attempt to know as God knows and to see as God sees. All human history by the deliberate purpose of God is touched by finitude and ignorance. There is no infallible revelation in terms of truths or facts which escapes the relativity of the human situation. We must all and ever be justified by faith in God beyond full seeing.

To be sure, fundamentalism in this sense means more an attitude of knowing that precludes trust and charity than it does the mere content of faith. In actuality, people often live their faith differently from the framework of doctrine within which they live. When I was an immigrant boy, freshly in America with no family or financial backing, I was taken seriously ill. A saintly churchwoman, a perfect stranger to me, took me into her home and nursed me back to health. One day, many years later, she heard me make a remark about some uncharitable judgments of the fundamentalists. She stopped me.

"Nels," she challenged, "what is a fundamentalist?"

I began to define fundamentalism in the above manner, but she shook her head and said:

"Nels, I am a fundamentalist!"

That was true. A great person, charitable and loving, she yet held on to the inerrancy of the Bible in such a simple and direct trust in God that the Bible never came between God and her. And was not my own mother, beloved of God and of those who knew her, doctrinally a fundamentalist? Yet how far she moved from any critical attitude of those who did not share her views, and how ready she was to accept all who "loved the Lord."

Thus in speaking of fundamentalism, our aim is to point up the contrast between an attitude of self-sufficient knowledge in the Bible and a central and open trust that seeking, finds, and yet knows its deep poverty of knowledge, especially as an intention toward life. Those who think they know all the answers have no living faith.

To be sure, the definiteness of direction that marks both Islam and fundamentalism is a strong asset. A narrow, dogmatic faith demands an unquestioning allegiance and generates a zealous relation with regard to rival faiths, both defensively and offensively. Besides, it structures the inner life and helps deliver its worshipers from confusion. But such false faith does not move. It is fixed. It does not provide a forward dynamic of the spiritual life. It never explores far beyond its narrow boundaries. It is the false faith of the static life based on sight.

Both modern education and modern history have undermined fundamentalism. Those who, consequently, have had true faith burst in on them can no longer allow themselves to be fenced in by such static dogmatism. They must find the faith that moves.

Similarly creedalism is the blocking of faith; it is a reason for the disappearance of faith. Creedalism is an attempt at concentrated sight. It is a valiant effort by the community of faith to preserve its purity. As a statement of faith, held merely as the report of community experience regarding the way, a creed can be of help. It can even become the basis for further creative formulation. But held as factual truth for worshipers to believe on external authority, the creed becomes the occasion for stagnation, for ready-made sight, for possession of the final answers.

Creedalism as having the final answers is fixation of faith. For congregations to stand up Sunday after Sunday to repeat that they believe a ready-made sight, which as a matter of fact they do not see, and the factualness of which most of the mumblers subscribe to only with reservations—except, of course, insofar as they are precritical or uncritical and have not yet risen to the level of faith—encourages basic dishonesty and stands in the way of faith. Christianity is justification by faith and not by sight, by God and not by creed. There can be little doubt that few arrangements have more seriously undermined and even prevented true faith than has creedalism. Creedalism, I repeat, is the concentrated attempt to live by sight and not by faith.

Roman Catholicism likewise strives to live by sight and not by faith. It claims an infallible revelation entrusted to an infallible church. Both the objective and the subjective visions are guaranteed. Men are asked to trust an infallible historic event and an infallible human agency. An infallible person was infallibly incarnated without human father and within an infallible mother, a woman born without sin. This person gave us an infallible revelation and founded an infallible organ of interpretation which even finally received an infallible head in history.

This great church, in many respects noble and good for our confused times, nevertheless at its heart practices the idolatry of sight rather than offering the organ of faith. It has final answers and tells final answers, not only of dogma but for much of life. Therefore, in spite of its numerous true believers who go beyond the central confines, the Roman Catholic Church generates childishness rather than childlikeness.

Childishness is simple acceptance of parental direction, without personal maturation based on the child's own questioning. The wise parent never gives all the answers. He lets the child grow into creative discovery. Wise parents point directions and help to inspire motivation. They help provide dynamic for movement. The Catholic Church aims basically at sight, a perfect revelation interpreted infallibly by an historic church, and not at faith, the personal and communal

trust in God beyond all final knowledge. For this reason it
neither inspires moral vigor nor spurs to intellectual creativity
where it dominates most successfully, thus becoming easy
prey for Communist totalitarianism. Many who turn Communist are simply exchanging what seems to them a more
plausible and profitable childishness for the older one of their
church.

Liberalism by its primary stress on reason also aimed mostly
at sight. Seeing is supposed to be believing, but what one
really sees or really knows one does not believe. In order to be
faith, believing must go beyond seeing. It may be argued that
liberalism had faith in human reason, or in the scientific
method. Such faith, to be sure, in proper measure and with
right use, is commendable, but it is not religious faith. Religious faith ventures beyond such seeing. Liberalism tended to
turn religion into philosophy or science and to trust in education as its method of perpetuation and extension. Faith begins
where reason cannot see. Faith faces choices which reason
cannot settle. The fabric of religious meaning and morality
was torn to shreds when liberalism demanded that both be
validated like philosophy or science. Both rest in man's creative outreach, in his enduring as seeing the invisible, in his
inner heart of faith. Liberalism, in seeking valid directon, tried
to prove a goal beyond its reach, and, failing, left man meaningless and without moral stamina.

As a personal confession I have to admit my life's deepest
frustration. Out of the depths of suffering over many years
came the vision of Christian truth. I saw, as if transfigured,
the whole of human experience and meaning illuminated and
solved within a fuller reach of the central meaning of God as

sovereign love, when alien philosophies had been eliminated, and Christianity interpreted creatively within its own philosophical framework. Overwhelmed with joy within all my sufferings I worked year after year, producing book after book to share my vision, believing that each new book would surely break down the resistance to, and the ignoring of, God's glorious, saving truth.

After twenty years of trying, I began to wither. I could not deny the truth I had seen, but neither could I deny that it was not generally wanted. Knowing that I had no right to grow bitter, but only better, I examined my vision in critical self-appraisal. After long seeking, I think I see my trouble. I, too, had sought to cure the world's ills by seeing, by knowledge. As a pointing of direction within faith, my work can still be of use. But if it should be accepted as ready-made answers for others to swallow as final knowledge, I should have done faith a disservice.

What I had done, then, was to believe that knowledge would cure our ills. But such knowledge of ultimates, as knowledge, however true, would take the place of faith. It would rob us, in effect, of our human finitude; it would steal from us the freedom that roots in real risk, in not seeing. Finding demolishes faith. Man's original sin is the seeking to see as God sees; to know good and evil as God knows them. Man does not need to know as God knows, but he needs to trust God within the failures of his sight as well as the sin of his life. Man above all else needs to trust the love of God.

Precisely the love of God, the heart of my theology, cannot be made into a philosophy. To make the love of God into a new philosophy is to kill it as faith. The use of theology as sight, and not as a servant of faith, constitutes a most subtle but also a most dangerous heresy. From now on I intend never to push the truth that I see as knowledge, but instead to commend it as faith, by interpreting it, of course, but even more by the living of it. There lies our need. This distinction between faith and knowledge is the reason that Socrates, Buddha, and Jesus could so mightily help the world without writing books. They gave general directions for faith but never supplied all the answers of knowledge. They were therefore primarily religious and effective.

III

True faith suffers no fixation; but neither, on the other hand, is it fugitive. It moves ahead toward a goal that is definite enough in direction to be inviting, but at the same time indefinite enough to demand flexibility of search. It is like a fascinating mountain peak that lures the climber but also compels him to choose his way over and over again. Faith is not like scientific prediction. It can be guided by no automatic compass. Nor is faith like propositional truth, requiring fixed meaning.

Faith is, rather, like life. A sure sign of intelligence is flexibility of adjustment. No individual can know his future in detail, no matter how much he plans. He is brought up in a home where situations as well as people change. However carefully he chooses a mate, he cannot really know her intimately until he lives with her. And the "feel" of life is ever different and ever new. Life never repeats itself exactly.

Some, to be sure, live in a rut. They are afraid of life and therefore refuse new experiences as much as possible. They live the safely tried routine, constantly shutting out the frightening new invitations to opportunity. The more they succeed, the less faith they have in life. The more they have their way, the less life they find. Fearing life, they shrink from it, and succeeding well in their fixation suffer from life's impoverishment and monotony.

Others do not so much sit out the dance of life in their lonely, safe corner as run away from life. They are fugitives. They flee life in the seeming search for it. They are afraid of every present and seek an imaginary future. They find no fixed goal at all to direct them. Whatever they are doing is unsatisfactory and they seek continually for that better day which they know should be theirs. Therefore they never stick to any task. They shift from position to position, or from place to place. They live the fugitive life. These fugitives have no more faith in life than those who suffer from fixation of faith. They substitute some dream of life for its waking reality. They, too, shun real life.

Faith in life calls for flexibility. Such faith accepts life as it is for the better. It is neither afraid of the new nor enamored of it. People with such faith neither leave their letters unopened out of fear nor ache for the mail to arrive. They live in the present. When the new comes into the present they assess it and respond constructively toward it, whether for use or dismissal. They suffer from no fixation but neither are they driven by fugitiveness.

Much failure of faith, in any case, comes from lack of flexibility. Dogmatism is fixation of faith. Dogmatism is worship of the God of the past at the expense of the living God.

Doctrines are travel reports from previous voyagers on the sea of life. When one set of doctrines is selected as alone leading to the goal, whereas countless others have indicated that they have proceeded with some success along quite different lines, ancestor worship is taking the place of divine worship.

Theology is the study of God. All of us have a theology. Therefore, merely to attack theology as the cause of the fixation of faith is wrong. But more and more it grows apparent that theology can become mostly the accumulation of the past on the present, smothering living faith. Theology should not build fences as it develops, to hedge in future travelers, but should rather from its experience erect clear road signs. By so doing, both dangers of fixation and fugitiveness would be lessened. There is help for direction, but each new generation is free to find the faith that serves its need.

Faith, then, is movement with direction, neither fixed nor fugitive. It is direction of life with intelligent openness to the new. It is power both to continue and to make adjustment. The trouble with any figure of speech, however, is that it is external to the situation itself and never quite speaks to it. Life is not a road which every generation travels in the same way. It is a road similar enough in nature so that each new generation can learn something in general from the past. But fortunately it is sufficiently unlike so that no generation has ever gone its particular road before. It is therefore no mere continuation of the past. Life is ever in some sense a new creation.

Thus there can never be mere accumulation of insight. Those who know the tracks of the past the best are often the least fitted to try the untrodden road. Otherwise fixation would be a virtue. The new would simply be a repetition or at most an extension of the past. But neither is life a matter of mere newness. Those who have learned little from those who have gone before also present scant offerings in terms of pioneering. Creativity is never the product of fugitiveness. It is rather the achievement of flexibility. True faith means a steady pursuit of the goal, using signposts from the past, but with creative inventiveness for the future.

Even science, for instance, works with the unknown. Today it works also with invisibles, like genes and atoms. Scientific research has a genuine goal, based on what has been learned up to the present time. The researcher should know as much as possible of this past. But in finding the new he must often reformulate the old. Not that it was simply wrong, but that past results had to be corrected in the light of new findings.

The scientist needs faith in the unknown that it can become known, in the past that it can be directive in the search, and in the present that both the known and the unknown can be better known so as to be corrected and discovered. Such a mind-set suffers neither from fixation nor fugitiveness but is flexibly free and effective.

William James's autobiography discloses him as a strange combination of fugitiveness and flexibility. He never was happy where he was. While living in Europe he dreamed of America. As soon as he set foot in the United States he began planning his return to the Continent. Yet while in either place he lived, learned, and appropriated in richness of experience more than most people who stay longer. Or he was continually resigning his professorship at Harvard for a felt lack of knowledge. He felt uncertain, insecure, unworthy of his post. Particularly he felt that he never knew books enough to teach at Harvard; and yet out of his reading and thinking came the occasion for the subsequent studying of his works by the generations. His fugitiveness drove him on, but he never lacked goal in general; thus he lived a flexible faith. Few have been more open than he in their faith, even though they perhaps had steadier aim.

Christian revelation is no substitute for faith. It should be instead the occasion for faith. Meaning should direct ahead even while mystery should obscure the fuller seeing. Indeed, Christian revelation is of a flexible life, inviting and formed enough to elicit response, and yet deep and hidden enough to preclude knowledge, except as the past is actually appropriated within the experience of living itself.

Consider the words that give content to Christian revelation. Christ means God's kind of life, God's kind of love, God's kind of spirit, offered for our lives, as their basis and power. We all know in general what life, love, and spirit are, but how utterly, unreachably deep they all go in their possibilities, and how fast they recede in their fullness from our own concrete lives! We know these realities most intimately, and yet they are still most strange. Just so, that revelation is the nearest to us that is ever the hardest to reach.

Perhaps a concrete experience can suggest how such duality is possible. A young father was driving along the Wilbur Cross Parkway in the beautiful hills of Connecticut with his small daughter in the front seat, when suddenly a large mountain loomed and the highway appeared to end.

"Look!" said the father. "There's no road over the mountain; we are going to go right through it!"

The little girl laughed in unbelief, but as they drove nearer and nearer she became visibly uneasy. Yet she trusted her father in that half-believing childlike manner. Then suddenly the astonished child saw a tunnel opening, and they did go right through the mountain! A way had been prepared for them.

Faith is keeping on toward the mountain of mystery, following whatever trail leads on in its direction. The road that leads through that mountain cannot be seen from afar. The road becomes visible only as the traveler reaches it. Too much seeing prevents true faith. Man actually cannot see the tunnel, let alone through it, until he reaches it. The tunnel of truth as well as the tunnel of death each person and each generation must ever pass through anew. All assurances are encouraging, but all attempts at premature seeing are vain.

True faith is no fixation nor is it fugitive, but it is direction and movement with flexibility. True faith does not see all the answers. Its finality is not of knowledge but of trust. Only faith makes faith final.

2: The Finding of Faith

If all of us have to live by faith of some kind, the problem is obviously how to find the right faith. For some, such a search means whatever faith gives the fullest personal satisfaction. For others, the striving for faith is the same as the striving for truth and reality. For most, and for all in some degree, the pursuit of a living faith which drives all people involves a combination of satisfaction and truth.

Satisfaction has to do with the whole person. No isolated function of the self, like reason, will, or feeling, alone can satisfy the self. But the whole person is far more than ever his conscious personality. Each person lives most deeply below the level of his conscious choices, yes, below conscious awareness. He is linked with the long past of mankind in terms of archetypal drives which are subconsciously structured in the total racial consciousness. He is linked, too, with his own total past in terms of patterns of response which run

[22

far below his understanding of them at any one time.

Somehow satisfaction can go deep into experience only when this depth dimension of the self is satisfied. Therefore no faith can really hold full sway over the personality which is not rooted in the total past of its community. Especially important are the experiences of early life, both in family living and in the most elemental social relationships of the concrete childhood community. No faith will prove adequate that is not genuinely and fulfillingly related to each man's primitive experience, in the sense of his primary archetypal backgrounds.

But faith, we remember, is man's response to life in what Tillich calls "the dimension of depth." It is man's evaluative reaction to his whole world, far below his merely intellectualistic conceptions of religion or his merely conscious willing in regard to the world. Faith deals with the ultimate. Faith has to do with God. Since religion is mostly communal both in origin and in present practice, no personal faith can fully meet the deepest needs of the self apart from its relation to the communal background.

I

Faith's first problem in finding satisfaction, therefore, is the right appropriation of its heritage. At the very least man's faith must be rightly related to his heritage. Without proper appropriation of faith's heritage man suffers from a rootless religion. Faith must be firmly rooted. Like a plant in the garden it will not grow unless it is correctly planted in man's true heritage.

Any gardener has seen people set out strong young stock only to have the plants wither and die because they were never tightly packed into the soil, while others have taken weaker specimens and made them live and grow by their planting the young flowers firmly into the right soil. How disastrous air pockets can be at the roots of a newly planted rosebush! Each plant should be set out not only deeply enough but with firm rootage.

Countless people suffer from a rootless faith. They are religious without deep and firm rootage. It is tragic to see people who have been converted from one religion to another, but whose emotional roots still reach for the soil from which they come. A Japanese Christian from a Buddhist background can feel himself into depth satisfactions through a Noh play. Even Christian professors of Hindu background may argue from the depths of being that belief in astrology has actually proved of life-and-death importance to them or to intimate acquaintances.

Many of us will recognize this experience from within our own backgrounds. A fundamentalist may turn Unitarian, but the emotional structure he carries with him makes him not a relaxed liberal but a zealous "fundamentalist" Unitarian. A Baptist may change his denomination as a young man and live the rest of his life in a new atmosphere. And yet he knows that he is never fully at home in the new setting. Even though he may not be able to endure some externals of faith dear to the Baptists and therefore never fully belong there either, nevertheless he understands the feeling from within, he is "instinctively" at home there, and he can communicate among the Baptists with a depth ease which fails him elsewhere.

Such dislocation because of rootlessness may, however, characterize a whole section of the community. I attended a service in a Japanese Christian church where the congregation were celebrating ancestors' day in their own adaptation of the Buddhist festival. At the front of the sanctuary was displayed a row of photographs of church members who had died, some recently, some in years past. As each name was called, the family or a representative would go forward, bow deeply toward the picture in dignified Japanese style, stand reverently for a few moments in honoring meditation, and bow again as in leave-taking, before returning to their seats. Such a service filled a deep, common human need, to be sure, but it meant much more than this. It was a genuine attempt at the recognition and acceptance of the communal past out of which the people had come. Somehow this simple service seemed more real and rewarding than much worship of a more distinctly Christian nature.

To be sure, the service also drew upon the feelings of nationalism that tend to enter into faith on more than a superficial level. Nationalism incorporates depths of common unconscious background and provides people with communal at-homeness. The Christian congregation held this service while the Buddhists were celebrating their special day for honoring their ancestors. Even on the level of general communal experience in the present, the small Christian community by means of its own ancestor celebration became part of the larger community and escaped a sense of isolation. Faith thus lay hold on far wider reaches than the merely personal or even the small sectional community. But beyond nationalism and the relation of minority to dominant culture there was still that depth reach into the common past that cannot be reduced to present response. Faith is never strong unless it is firmly planted in heritage. It cannot grow strong without roots that nourish.

Estrangement from heritage may characterize a whole age. We are living through a long era when we seem to be able neither to believe nor to reject the Christian faith. Intellectuals have long been telling us that the Christian era is over. Modern science, they say, has spelled the finish once for all of supernaturalism. Supernaturalism has become synonymous with superstition. But what is supernaturalism if not faith in a final order other than and more than nature? Anyone who genuinely believes in God the Creator is a supernaturalist! We may hedge at terms and shy away from words. But the problem is not words. It is the nature of faith itself. Can an honest, competently educated modern man any longer believe in a Supreme Being who created, orders, and will finally judge the world? Numberless strong leaders of thought simply assume that the Christian era of world history has come to its close.

But our need for faith was never greater and our people have never flocked as now to houses of worship. Church giving and building soar. And yet most people are troubled in spirit. They are uprooted. They cling to faith, but in their deeper and more honest moments they do not quite know what they believe. And our young people have generally pronounced Christianity a failure to stop war, corruption, and mental illness. They may still come along to church, for lack of other forms of faith, but they are not convinced of the Christian faith. The case is the same with the youth of other religions.

Faith always becomes verbalized. It has to become articulated in order to be perpetuated and shared. Faith does not live on rational truths. Faith must lay hold on symbols, stories, and events which represent not only the whole of life, but life in its deeper dimensions. Today there is general uneasiness about the articulation. Our theologies fail to satisfy people. They read with interest, and sometimes a passion that is almost pathetic, book after book on religion; but the books stimulate without quenching the aching thirst.

It might seem that the trouble is with trust in statements. Statements are descriptive of facts and not the living experience of choice and commitment. Statements fall short of dynamic; they do not move into the inner recesses of reality. I cannot forget how in Marburg, Germany, I had been reading intensively and struggling long with the truth of religion as this was battled back and forth in books. Then in the beautiful early Gothic Saint Elisabeth's Church I was confronted with an ancient crucifix. As I stood before it, the cosmic meaning of the Cross, the suffering heart of God, not only moved me but actually spoke reality to me at a depth far beyond any book.

Near the crucifix I saw the sarcophagus of an old Teutonic knight. In commissioning the sculpture, he had directed that on top of the sarcophagus he be portrayed reclining as a knight in armor, in the full splendor of the Order as he had been in life, but that directly below and as if within the casket a statue be made to represent his naked and decaying body being fed upon by toads and snakes. The sculptor's task was performed with realistic, if not with morbid, imagination! The combined effect of the crucifix and the sarcophagus was for me a cosmic experience. Here I saw life not only in its dimensions of earthly seriousness and deathly destruction but also in the light of the suffering God towering above both. Somehow the symbols grasped hold of life the way mere words did not.

To say, however, that symbols or myths can do what words cannot is sheer evasion. The depths of mystery could not speak at all unless they themselves were against a background of meaning. The problem of our age is not lack of communication. The trouble lies with the faith itself. Faith cannot be strong unless in some way it is planted in heritage. Can there be a common human heritage so deep that it will fulfill any specific proliferation of it? If faith cannot live strongly without deep roots, can faith be transplanted into a new soil that contains the valuable qualities of the old and yet is still better for it to grow in? Must finding faith be a return to a specific heritage and the fuller appropriation of it? Or can faith find a heritage so universally related to human history that it can still satisfy and offer even fuller satisfaction? Or can faith create its new symbols that both appropriate the heritage and yet satisfy present experience beyond every past? Such is surely the problem of heritage in relation to history.

II

Faith must be planted in heritage, but it must also be watered in history. Heritage without history is like a stagnant pool, with no fresh water flowing through it. By history we mean present living, the actual combination of continuing and changing the past, or that mixture of renewing the past and the creation of the new in the present. History is re-creation and creation. There is no history that is not for the most part heritage; but no heritage makes history by itself. The heritage must be appropriated in history, the past must be absorbed and reconstituted by the present.

For some people history is mostly heritage. Conservativism worships the past and tries to preserve it unchanged. The greatest need for conservativism is whenever history is changing the most rapidly. In times of flux there is special need for form. Today there is a strong turn to conservativism because of the bewildering changes that threaten even civilization itself. This turn is not only understandable but generally needed, for a rootless age threatens us, an era of drift, with frantic experimentation to meet unexampled rates of transformation. Because by our very situation our history cannot be mostly heritage, we grasp frantically for it.

But some eras prepare for our kind of shifting and nearly shiftless age. And some strands of the population are the builders of cataclysmic changes. There are some people who so worship the past that they fail to make the needed adjustment in each present. In this case heritage paralyzes history. Certain self-termed patriotic organizations so bask in the national heritage as to cripple thereby present history.

The founding of the United States was the result of creative vigor and daring. It came out of vision and enterprise. The hope of a few became history never to be forgotten and always to be honored. But the hope which our founding fathers turned into daring history has now become our heritage for our appreciation and inspiration. Some, however, try to preserve this heritage rather than use it to inspire the present. They try to freeze history. Perhaps by birth they may share a certain prestige and power, or think they do. They may therefore feel that true American history means the preservation of our original heritage: white, Anglo-Saxon, Protestant America. For this reason they glorify this heritage and try to burden history with it.

An attempt to preserve the heritage rather than to cultivate it may also result in an overall conservativism that resists all change. Our country now is the product of multiracial, multinational, multireligious, and multicultural backgrounds. Therefore our only true history is in the incorporation of all these drives into a creative, living present. A slow, observant trip around the world can make the traveler come home to see the beauty and the glory of our many-stranded homeland. Throwback organizations become divisive and paralyzing by their repudiation of the total heritage and by the suffocating influence of their static deification of their partial heritage. Besides, such narrow-minded partisans deaden history by a false conservativism that repudiates a constant, creative acceptance of the present and adjustment to its demands.

On the other side, we find irresponsible pressers for immediate change, whose hopes have no appreciation of heritage. Living in an unstructured future, unrelated to the pesistent forms from the past, they offer no valid creativity; their hope is fugitive. Every great reform is mostly the reforming of the past, the reshaping of it. Most of the present is always the past. Necessarily each present, in order to satisfy, must accept this basic fact. Radicals are usually rootless even though the literal meaning of the name "radical" implies going to the roots of things. For most people radicals are those who want big changes fast, too fast for soundness and safety. But there is also another use of the word which is more true to the literal meaning.

Some people call the superconservatives who write tracts and who picket progressive thinkers radicals. This usage appears to be turned upside down, but actually it is more true to the meaning of the word. In religion, too, we have the conservatives who cling desperately to the past and countenance no change. They are far more interested in roots than in fruits; they have little concern for the new flowers. Cut deep enough back toward the root and often we undercut the graft only to have the long-labored rose revert to primitive bramble. By worshiping heritage these "radicals" forfeit history. By their unwillingness to make any small, creative changes they lay the way open for the big battles and the dislocating and uprooting changes.

We also see, on the other hand, those whose hopes fail their heritage and therefore fail to create satisfactory history. Heritage cannot take the place of history. Faith planted in heritage must also be watered in history. No faith can satisfy the self or the community that does not go deep enough into the racial, communal, and personal background to lay hold on the archetypal structures which demand attention. But history demands equally the acceptance of the creative situation of the present. Each present is under the demand of the dimension of depth. It confronts the ultimate ever anew. It cannot keep feeding on stale meanings. The present cannot be effectively fed by even the most vigorous chewing of the cud of the past. The present calls for a new experience of right relations, a fresh and free confrontation of God's way with the world.

Both individuals and social groups, as well as society as a whole, must face this dynamic demand of history. Man must not forsake the heritage of the past nor may he accept it

without creatively appropriating it. How such use of the past
and reformulation of the present shall be carried out man cannot learn from the past. Therefore both man and mankind, to
live satisfactorily, must live by a lively hope.

III

Heritage is hope that has been realized. History is hope
being realized. There is no true history without heritage, but
hope always transcends both heritage and history. Hope is the
spring of faith. True faith lives by being planted in heritage,
watered in history, but grown by hope.

Our own concrete heritage is the Christian faith. Our history springs out of the presuppositions of the Christian faith:
God the Creator; God the Ruler of nature and history; God
who sent his Son to reveal himself and to save us; God the
fulfiller of human history beyond death. Human history is as
serious as decision and growth, but meaning centers in eternity
surrounded by mystery.

Our longer heritage of nearly two thousand years, however,
is complicated by a new, strong strand of inheritance, namely,
the scientific method and mood: the fact-centered, earth-
bound approach to truth and life that description gives. The
scientific age has itself evolved through many changes, and
especially in our day it is undergoing rapid and drastic transformation; but apart from the fear of our times of crisis that
has occasioned the rebirth of faith, or at least the desperate
search for it, the scientific aura has both deepened and spread.
For multitudes, science or the reports of science through
general education has actually become the dominant religion.

Their faith has taken as truth what a science-dominated education has taught them.

Modern Western man is generally caught between these two heritages: Christian faith and the scientific method. Contemporary history proceeds within the conflict between the two. Numberless people have never faced the conflict concretely because they have stayed mostly within the one heritage or the other. They are precritical of the situation, although in some way all modern life is touched by it. But if they are educated, they have somehow to come to terms with the relation between the two.

There are four main lines of choice. One chooses to preserve the heritage of the Christian faith as far as possible in its original form. Those who make this choice are the true conservatives. The name that comes closest both to the facts and to the attitudes of this position is fundamentalist. In general, they draw the battle line at the plenary inspiration of the Bible. Some of them are rigid and insist on a literal inspiration, even to the length of the days of creation or the biblical story of the ax floating on the river, or the sun actually standing still during a battle. Others make minor adjustments and rationalizations in order to feel more justified in maintaining their supreme loyalty, thus accepting the fact that the Bible is historically conditioned, admitting minor discrepancies but no major error or undependable portion. From within this loyalty the fundamentalists will generally, although not always, fight those who listen with more than a polite nod to the modernity of the rival heritage.

On the opposite extreme there are multitudes, especially in Europe but increasingly in the United States as well, who simply can no longer honestly hold on to what they call Christian ideology. For them, the Christian faith is hopelessly entangled in an outmoded supernaturalism, which for modern man can be nothing but superstition. For this reason, they have left the churches and have no active affiliation with them. Countless others keep on attending church because it is "the thing to do" and because they feel empty without it, even though they see the Christian faith either as an oppressive heritage of judgment that awakens guilt in them, or as a beautiful myth which they have outgrown. For some this is a relief, for others a hurting loss; but Christian ideology can no longer command their convictions.

A third group, led by great prophets like Karl Barth, insist that modern man can accept competently and honestly both heritages and turn them into creative history. Neither Christianity nor science when rightly understood, they contend, gives a world view. But God has shown himself once for all in Jesus Christ, especially in the actual raising of Christ from the dead. The central Christian fact is a matter of faith, not dependent upon human learning. For the facts of this world, including even the Bible as a book, this group accepts scientific knowledge. Theology is the science of God's mighty self-revelation in Christ as it describes the witness of faith. Human science cannot gainsay this fact, and all other facts, including even man's craving for immortality, we can leave to science. The Christian faith announces what God has done for the world in Christ and is doing now for us—offering us the incredible faith of God's "yea" in Christ against all natural evils and human fears. The third position thus makes a strong bid somehow to turn the two heritages into creative history.

A fourth group believe with the second that the Christian world view is dead for modern man and that it cannot be raised to life again. Led by great spirits and thinkers like Paul Tillich and Rudolf Bultmann, they are convinced that the scientific heritage is neither our hope nor our doom. While accepting the demise of the Christian faith in its original ideology at the hand of science, they nevertheless believe that the secret of salvation, for Bultmann, and the secret of both truth and salvation, for Tillich, have been found once for all in Jesus as the Christ. Although modern man can no longer believe in the personal God who created and rules the world, nor in a literal Incarnation, nor, of course, in any life after death, nonetheless in Jesus, or faith's picture of him, we can see the truth of the unconditional nature of the ground and goal of being and obtain the power for the fulfillment of life, by grace and faith, within the actual evils and tragedies of life. The Christian faith must be translated and transvaluated in terms of man's most stringent modern knowledge, but in terms also of the inner victories offered by what to this group is the heart of the Christian faith, namely, the conclusive fact of Jesus as the Christ, the existential truth of the Cross and the Resurrection.

The third and fourth responses of faith for history regarding our actual heritages have much in common. The basic difference is that the third group holds on to the actual reality of the transcendent God and to the literal Incarnation and Resurrection of Jesus Christ. But there are a few of us who believe that none of these four positions will do, that there has to be a far more serious and profoundly creative confrontation between the two heritages for a new creative synthesis to emerge, without sacrifice of either honesty or competence. But such a work is radical and far-reaching to the point where the acceptance of it will necessarily meet strong resistance. The length of the resistance will depend upon the quality of the positive work and the degree of cataclysmic threat that may speed up all changes. In such a synthesis both heritages will have to undergo radical revision without sacrifice of essential truth.

But if the faith planted in heritage and watered in history is to grow in hope, faith must see the total situation it must face. Today's world complicates the task of faith by introducing into our knowledge with increasing intimacy the total heritage of the faiths of the world. More and more people are examining the offer made by other religions. No hope can be well founded that looks away from the offer of faiths that have lived even longer than ours and have given a steadiness and general peace to their adherents over the millennia.

At this point we shall surely experience the three kinds of attitudes which we described in our first chapter. Some will have a fixation on the Christian faith and refuse to examine any other offer. They will be stuck in the rut of their own past. Others will give the romantic response of a fugitive faith. They will leave their heritage to hasten to the new, which precisely by its newness must be better. They will hanker for a fresh faith, but having cut the root of their growth, they will wither, unless they succeed in taking root in the new soil, and after long watering and growth may possibly again flourish and bear fruit within a new setting. Such cases there are, but they are rare and generally brittlely defensive or wistfully aggressive.

Those who realize with serious responsibility that modern man has now to live beyond his own two heritages in order to make adequate history, will have to grow in hope by openly understanding and evaluating these new sources of our history. They will have a rootage in their own religion, be creatively aware of their own two heritages, but also be flexible as to the appearance of new religious offers. They will neither dismiss the new because of a sterile fixation nor accept the new because of a fugitive craving for change, but they will move ahead in the direction set by their most authentic past, while all the time examining whether their general goal of faith cannot be made both richer and more precise by the new heritages which have come their way.

Thus does hope transcend both heritage and history. Hope scans the horizon for the fuller creative possibility. Faith grows by hope. In the next chapter we shall try to assess how faith, having found the resources for its creative work, to which this chapter pointed, can try to follow the leads of hope toward fulfillment. Faith has to have a focus in order to move ahead; this focus cannot be found apart from our concrete heritages, but faith can find fulfillment only as it dares to follow the hope that reaches beyond heritage and history.

3: Following Faith

Faith finds satisfaction and truth by following its focus. Faith moves toward goals it can envisage only generally. Faith is neither knowledge nor ignorance. Faith is pressing on beyond what has been seen, and in some respect and in some measure, even in spite of what it sees. Faith is movement toward goals of life that can never be either fully described or prescribed. The fulfillment of faith comes only in the movement and with each attainment. We experience the finality of faith as such as we travel within the heritage of the past, meeting the demands of the present, and pressing on toward the future.

Genuine faith is free because it transcends both the past and the present. It lives in hope. Faith's freedom lies in its not being bound by either the past or the present; indebted heavily to both and unable to live apart from either past or present, faith yet grows by creating history from within the resources not only of heritage and present history, but also of the boundless future. Faith creates the present out of the future. Each age must create history out of hope, using the material of heritage, but adding to it its own creation. Therefore faith stops being faith if it becomes sight. It is the substance of things hoped for, and not yet seen.

Today demands that the fullest faith, for us, relate itself to our two conflicting heritages and the further heritages brought into relevance from other faiths by the new accessibility of the whole world. Can faith sort out and evaluate its present hopes before assaying its creative work?

I

There are three main choices: those offered by Hinduism, Buddhism, and Christianity. To be free, faith must dare to examine these three main choices both openly and with commitment. It must dare to face the truth and commit itself to the best hope available. We have excepted Islam as not offering any major choice in itself. The truths of Islam can be found within Christianity, except for its witness against idolatry and for monotheism. At this latter point, to be sure, Christianity needs to heed its insistent demand. When we come to consider the Christian faith we must remember the truth contained in Islam's criticism of it.

Outside Christianity, the two main choices for faith today among the world religions are Hinduism and Buddhism. Both these religions are now missionary minded. Hinduism, at its highest, holds that true reality is good. This actual world and self as such are not true reality but *maya*, that is, a disastrous mixture of ignorance, suffering, and change. The essential self is the dimension in depth below these changes and sufferings, which is, in fact, one with essential reality. This essential reality, according to a major and high branch of Hinduism, is an indescribable ground of being, underlying all else and offering intelligence, being, and bliss. By transcending one's actual self, each person can find this ground of being and lose himself within it, thereby finding also his essential self.

Another main branch of Hinduism believes in a personal God of redemption who by grace offers life eternal, beginning in this life by identification with his will and deepening beyond death into the fuller union and communion with God.

This life, for both branches of Hinduism, is part of the endless reality of the spiritual realm, coming into birth and issuing in rebirth endlessly, except as the self gains the fulfillment of identification with the Ground of being or with Goc. Living is characterized throughout by justice. Each person always gets what he deserves either in this life or in the life to come. A person is his life, past, present, and future. He is his choices of knowledge, feeling, and work. Although the consequences do not follow the deeds directly, each person stores up for himself a sure harvest, for good or for ill. Freedom is real and serious. Heritage keeps entering history even while hope offers the better day.

But our desires are so strong for immediate satisfaction, and our reason so blinded by our desires, that almost invariably we keep choosing our selfish enjoyment rather than the good, the true, and the beautiful which can deliver us into newness of life. We do not have to do so, however, and some at times go far beyond ordinary life. Especially important for release from the wheel of actual life is desireless duty. In this state all knowledge, feeling, and willing go beyond our cravings and are acts performed within identification with the essential self and reality, which lie beyond the realm of personal desires.

Reality in itself, then, is good, and can be attained by the way of knowledge, the way of love, or the way of disciplined work; but these means are only preparatory, for reality finally grasps the self beyond all self-help.

All religions, according to Hinduism, seek the same goal. They seek it against different backgrounds and by means of differing symbols, but essential reality is one. Even to call religion "Hinduism" is to introduce division. We are what we are, and must accept and help one another. What divides are our ingroup ideas and narrow loyalties; not the goal, but our insistence that we alone are on the right road or have the right road.

Some modern Hindus, like Radhakrishnan, stress strongly that God is sovereign love, that his love must eventually fulfill and perfect each person in eternity, but that what lies beyond such perfection, beyond such personal fulfillment, man cannot now know. We can only trust and believe, work for one another with integrity and concern, and leave all else in the hands of God. Beyond God the Creator and Fulfiller lies the ungraspable Mystery where we can only adore, not define and argue.

So speaks high Hinduism, a religion of the ages, with amazing knowledge of psychology and of human nature in general. Its high tolerance and long patience, its stress on justice, freedom, and, beyond both, the ever-living hope of fulfillment

—not only according to the best we know but also far beyond
all knowledge—come as great mountain ranges of hope to
modern men who have not lost all feeling for the spiritual
realities that transcend this life.

Actual Hinduism, of course, contains much low religion
and superstition, but so do all religions in some measure!
There has been a lack of strong social concern in Hinduism,
but anyone who studies India can soon be overwhelmed by
the seeming impossibility of changing its conditions, and by
the need to find faith within and beyond the world. At its
highest, Hinduism is a faith of freedom and justice, of love
and acceptance, of eternal reality and the hope of salvation.

The fact that great "Christian" thinkers like Tillich basically espouse the high Hindu point of view, within a thoroughly reworked Christian terminology, may signal the sweep-
ing into world-wide power of this faith, which perhaps already
long before the Christian era had swept into Egypt and
Greece, and by way of Greek philosophy became a main in-
gredient in the original Christian heritage, or, at least, a side
source, as in Heraclitus' *logos* doctrine, in Stoicism, and in
Neoplatonism. No responsible thinker today, in any case, can
relegate the hope of Hinduism for faith either to India or to a
few scattered Ramakrishna missions. As the world, if it remains, becomes one, we shall have to listen to Hinduism as
we make our free choice.

The freedom of faith means the privilege of looking at all
hopes for history without anxiety and without a sense of guilt.
Faith, fettered to any past heritage, is not free. The history
that rejects any heritage available to hope is not free. The
freedom of faith involves the privilege of free search and of
responsible choice.

Another choice of basic nature in today's world is Buddhism. Some want to treat Buddhism as being of two kinds, the original "small vessel" variety and the later and larger "large vessel." The Mahayana Buddhists, or those of the expanded faith, called the original, or Theravada Buddhists, "small vessel," implying that they let themselves be limited by their original heritage. The fact is, however, that Buddhism at its root heritage is one. The so-called larger variety, or Mahayana Buddhism, is basically a return to Hinduism—without its cultural confinement, and with a mixture of other religions, including original Buddhism and perhaps Christianity—and a creative, concrete growth into numberless branches. The attempt on the part of some Mahayana Buddhists to claim original Buddhism as really intending its own later affirmations seems unfortunate and unfounded. The present-day revival of Theravada, or "small vessel" Buddhism, especially in Burma and Ceylon, although with some important dissension, goes back to the true Buddhist beginnings.

Whereas Hinduism offered its hope of essential reality, perfect beyond ignorance, suffering, and change, Buddhism starts with the truth of suffering. There is no essential reality beyond this desire-fettered world. Suffering is caused by desire. Escape comes only by the illumination that since desire is not real, suffering can be escaped as desire is destroyed. As long as desire reigns we must be born again into this life of desire; we are doomed to continue within it. When all desire is gone, however, man can become completely rid of the suffering self; the drive of desire which is life is blown out and is no more.

The wise man, according to Buddhism, does not dispute

about ultimates. He knows there is release from life. That is enough. He knows that there is no essential reality beyond this world. Therefore he does not argue abstractly against the existence of such a realm of transcendence, but rather avoids foolish discussion. Instead of discussing the situation he pulls the arrow out of his wound by means of such self-disciplines as will let the self accept the truth of deliverance. The means of salvation, the so-called eightfold path or the middle road of caring neither too much nor too little, are psychologically helpful on the way to release, but ultimately there is neither being nor meaning.

Some scholars want to interpret Buddhism as claiming ultimate reality beyond the negation of all that we can now know. Such an interpretation seems untrue to the founder; indeed, leading Theravada Buddhists today consider it to be a distortion of the teachings of original Buddhism. Buddhism claims that to be is to be partial and selfish, that such existence produces suffering, and that therefore escape from existence is man's highest hope. Such a faith appeals to much in modern man. If we share modern man's pessimism and despair about life and unless we believe that there is fulfillment in eternity beyond death, Buddhism can come both as realism and as the true wisdom of salvation.

Let us examine these religions in terms of self. Hinduism, as well as Buddhism, recognizes that this life consists of change, ignorance, and suffering, but holds that essential reality lies beyond or below such life of change. It contends that the self can come to know its essential nature, indeed, become identified with true being, and thus live fulfilled beyond the hurts and changes of this world. This world, deepest down, is unreality and has no intrinsic meaning or relation to true being.

Buddhism, on the other hand, knows that the self consists of a series of changes which fail to satisfy it and which engender suffering. The self consists in these changes and in their continuation one from the other. But none of these changes is real. The self is the desire for more of these fleeting experiences, for perpetuation of unsatisfying enjoyment, for an impossible attainment; but this self is not real, for beyond such changes there is no self. Therefore really to grasp this truth and thereby to become freed from desire is deliverance. Whereas Hinduism finds salvation by means of identification with the truth of essential being, Buddhism finds salvation in the truth of no being.

We can never evaluate the hopes for history until we explore also our own Christian heritage within its total past. Christianity also recognizes these changes, knows these drives of desire, and is well acquainted with the experience of suffering. Christianity holds, nevertheless, that the self is neither the perfect essential self below these changes, as Hinduism claims, nor without permanent being, as Buddhism holds, but is, rather, a potential in process. The self and the world are both God's creation for the purpose of perfecting the self. Suffering comes both from sin and from the frustrations of the self in its growth as it learns from its experience within nature and history. Thus the Christian heritage is vastly different from the Hindu and the Buddhist.

Our Western heritage is twofold: the Christian and the scientific; and the two are in conflict with each other. Today's world offers the two new hopes of Hinduism and Buddhism as important sidelines to our two main heritages. Faith, to be fully free, must be allowed to make a genuine choice. What then?

II

A free faith is always fresh. It keeps fresh by continually reliving its heritage in present history in the light of ever-new hopes. Every era has its peculiar hopes. The Christian faith has lived through a series of choices: Judaism, Platonism, Aristotelianism, Manichaeism, Neoplatonism, Islam, as well as modern rivals such as scientism, naturalism, and secularism and the non-Christian religions of the world. Faith, we recall, is planted in heritage, watered in history, but grown in hope. The hopes always go beyond or extend broader than any one faith. Not to want to look beyond heritage is to suffer fixation, while, on the other hand, to become romantic about the rivals is to treat faith fugitively. A faith that is flexible will cherish its heritage but at the same time dare to keep fresh by a free examination of all the hopes for history.

Some label such freedom the search for syncretism. But syncretism is lending an ear to all voices without power to decide for an organizing center, and hence is the failure of reworking the faith into an organic whole. On the very contrary, to observe all hopes for history as diverging heritages come into view, and to learn from them in maximum measure in order to enrich one's own faith, or indeed even to change the center of faith if need be, demands the kind of freedom which keeps faith fresh and real.

What can we learn, then, from non-Christian hopes for

history? From the heritage of science we observe that the forms in which all religions come partake of the time of their birth, and that the religions also incorporate elements from history as they grow, which later histories may find to be false hopes. There is always, therefore, a struggle on the part of any faith to keep authentic as the conflict rages ever anew between the worshipers of the past and its despisers, between those who take heritage without a transcending hope and those whose hopes never incorporate genuinely the needed truth of heritage.

Science is basically a descriptive method. In itself it provides no world view or metaphysical system. Instead it establishes facts, ingredients of any interpretation of the world. All world views are systems of faith. But even though science in itself produces no world view, scientists no less than philosophers and theologians do produce such interpretations. Usually the scientists have called their world views knowledge and have dignified their findings by means of their common acceptance within the educational activities of the age. The fact that science keeps changing its findings continually often makes the scientist forget that any total interpretation is a matter not so much of descriptive knowledge as an organization based on faith judgment.

To accept science as a faith is impossible; it is a method of finding facts. But in the light of these facts faith can criticize its own convictions. Granting the changing nature of scientific findings and the fact that it does not provide a world view, nevertheless modern man certainly has learned from science, for instance, that the cosmology of the biblical world view is outdated. Christians should also learn from science to be wary of all historical claims. Faith cannot live by knowledge, certainly not by historic knowledge in its mere pastness, for history affords no proofs. Therefore, the Christian faith lives neither by the biblical world view nor by its historic claims. At this point, both those who reject traditional Christianity outright and those who reinterpret it according to our best modern knowledge, like Tillich and Bultmann, are undoubtedly right. But neither can man live by mere tentativeness or by any collection of facts. The Christian faith at its heart, therefore, cannot be touched by either the scientific mood or method. From science Christianity can learn to reappraise and reorganize its faith, but science as such is no rival faith.

Scientism is an assumed scientific construction, but must be judged by both the critical and the creative reason as a faith, not as knowledge. When this fact becomes clear to modern man he can choose his faith far more intelligently. Scientism is usually some form of naturalism, or of making this world ultimate. As such it must be judged. Our age is the first for hundreds of years that has more and more deliberately turned its back on naturalism as unable to meet either the intellectual or the practical demands put upon it.

From Judaism and Islam Christianity should learn to repent of its central idolatry: its substitution, in effect, of Jesus for God, its making Jesus God.

Christianity was born in the power of the life and work of Jesus Christ. His life became interpreted with respect to both the transcendent, living God of Judaism and the incarnational *logos* idea that came out of Hindu-Greek origins. Such interpretation of God as both sovereignly and unimaginably in some sense beyond the world, and yet also working and being within it, is very likely the fullest interpretation of God available to man. Christianity in coming to birth used such sources as the living Personal God from the Hebraic background, but also related faith to Greek thought by stressing Spirit and Love, also present in the Hebraic heritage, as the means of God's immanence. No full separation, of course, can be made at any point between the two heritages, but there is a noticeable distinction of stress and of use. Such use of the total event of Jesus Christ was not only proper but consummatorily creative.

But instead of properly using the life of Jesus as the central symbol for interpreting God, thus seeing God in terms of Life, Person, Spirit, and Love, man's need to create gods made Jesus into a God, and shifted authority and loyalty generally from God to Jesus. Jesus became the effective God of the Christian faith. The window was taken for the view, God's personal Presence in Jesus as Spirit and Love for God himself. The tragedy is that the truest and best in our understanding of God and the critical example of God's life on earth were made into a myth that robbed the Christian faith of its potential universal nature as a world religion.

Judaism and Islam stand as permanent protests against such idolatry. However beautiful and well meant such faith may be, it nevertheless blocks man's full, immediate access to the God who in Jesus entered history in such a decisive manner as to give man a universal heritage and an inexhaustible hope. This mythmaking still goes on, now including even the mother of Jesus. Instead, the kind of life we meet in Jesus could be the way, the truth, and the life of God's nature, insofar as faith must commit itself, and of God's total relation to the world. The heritages both of science and of Judaism-Islam can thus help us to criticize our Christian heritage in order to disown whatever false histories we have appropriated and more nearly to accept only what is genuine.

What, then, can we learn from Hinduism and what from Buddhism? In general we can gather what all high religions have learned in their heyday or at their greatest power, that faith lives at its fullest only in its concern with ultimates. Both Hinduism and Buddhism reject ordinary experience as the standard for religious revelation. Deeper, above, beyond, within—by whatever figures—lies the ultimate truth that alone can satisfy. Religion is not basically of this world of change, however much it may be concerned with it or seek to escape from it. The ultimate has to do with the eternal, the invisible, the immeasurable, the inexpressible. It is the realm of the Spirit. Man's ground and goal lie not in our heritage, history, or hope, but in the eternal transcendence that man can never more than point at, that he can never control, and that he must indeed accept without reservation before he can be fulfilled.

Faith, therefore, Hinduism and Buddhism agree, can be satisfied only by faith; never by knowledge. Knowledge can help to steer faith, but when insight takes the place of believing, then truth is reduced to the measure of man and stands in the way of faith. In our days of glorifying the scientific approach and in our mood of the tentativeness of knowledge, we have to learn, as perhaps never before, that man cannot live by sight but must live by faith. Looking at these other faiths, Christianity can recover its own primacy of faith over against the many voices that try to discredit faith by reducing it to unprovable knowledge.

Secondly, we can learn from these religions that our earthly history is but a moment, not only in eternity, but in man's history as a creature. Christian ideology has traditionally worked with a cramped notion that man decides in this life for heaven or hell, for his eternal destinies. The moral truth, however obvious, that no finite sin, deep though it be, can deserve infinite punishment, has been too high for miniature theologies, "Christian" in name only, of invidious men. To the worshiping of a moral God they have preferred to possess the power to frighten sinners into the Kingdom, or to exult over their eventual downfall. They have magnified man's freedom to ruin God's purpose eternally at the expense of God's freedom not to be frustrated by his work. Hinduism and Buddhism can teach us at this point that God's pedagogy has endless time at its disposal and that his ways are dependable unexceptionally so that man is free to keep on in his own foolish and sinful way, until he starves and suffers enough to come to himself and to own up to his hopeless situation.

Those who have accepted the centrality of the God of love, moreover, need unimaginably long stretches to learn the fullness of the ways of God. Can man ever do so? Is there not an endless eternity of trying and finding, of newness within the inexhaustible resources of the eternal God? Certainly, to say that God's teaching program, his discipline, and his time for providing quiet and luxuriant growth of man's spiritual life are only in this earthly life is to make mockery of the fullness of God. If eternity means anything at all in terms of time and if creation here is serious in the first place, God's ways with men go on and on. This world is only God's beginning with us.

Hinduism and Buddhism believe in reincarnation, our re-birth into this life endlessly until we are ready to be fulfilled or released within the inexpressible Ultimate, whether of being or of nonbeing. Even though we cannot consciously remember the past, these religions maintain, we always live our heritage. History therefore becomes personally serious to the point of despair. Life usually becomes a burden; the wheel of rebirth, a constant threat. In such a situation religion naturally becomes man's most consuming interest. But for Hinduism and Buddhism, too, religion is primarily salvation for the fuller reality or from the burden of living.

Many Christians are now substituting reincarnation for the Christian doctrine of resurrection. I meet such Christians practically everywhere. There seems to me to be no ground for such shift in faith, however, except for those, of course, who believe that the only other alternative is eternal heaven and hell. But Christian faith can learn of the larger and longer teachings of God in worlds beyond this. Why should we have to be reborn into this world? Conscious memory and an enclosed selfhood may not be necessary for serious carry-over into life's continuation beyond death, but both seem more consistent with moral seriousness and good peda-gogy than do the Hindu and Buddhist views. Those of us who believe or are inclined to believe that God raised Jesus in some manner from the dead to communicate and inspirit his failing disciples, observe how complicated the matter of recognizable continuity even on the part of Jesus' most intimate friends can be, and ponder whether resurrection was a return to this earthly life for a purpose of communication. How much more difficult the question is when shifted to another existence, the concrete nature of which we cannot even fancy!

One possibility for faith to consider is God's use of the countless planets, on which some of our sanest astronomers now believe there is life, to foster further the children of his creation. If God uses these planets, he can indeed separate us all according to our response to his pedagogy. Some may go to the kind of environment of suffering and hardship that will make impossible the kind of freedom of rejection which this life offers. There may be countless such planets differing in conditions according to the needs of those sent there. And there may be countless unimaginable planets for our growth and fulfillment. Those who have grown spiritually close in this life may have the satisfaction of companionship, with conscious memory and joy, on the other side. Certainly such possibility was long ago envisaged by Nicholas of Cusa and has a strong tradition, culminating in the mighty thoughts on the subject of Immanuel Kant.

But such speculation can be at best suggestive. Why be reborn into time and space at all? The eternities may have resources for learning to accept God and to grow in his love that from our knowledge cannot even be fancied at its outermost edges. Therefore all thinking on this subject must remain centrally symbolic. It points to conditions rather than to places. We can believe that what lies beyond this earthly life in terms of God's further teaching and unfolding of his endless riches is consistent with his wisdom and his love, but cannot finally be spelled out by us within this life.

Perhaps anything we can know of the billions of galaxies is no more, comparatively speaking, than what an inframolecular occurrence could fathom if beyond its own infinitesimal segment of reality and even though it could never dream of any reality as large as a pinhead, it could glimpse the fact that reality was vast beyond its own measure to grasp. Our own measure of truth and reality can be no more than a confident guess into the illimitable ultimates; all we dare to believe is that the faithfulness of truth and concern that we witness and symbolize as the Christ reaches into the heart of the ultimate in such a way that we can trust far beyond all seeing, and expectantly await the unimaginable unfolding of the eternities.

One thing seems certain: scientific naturalism and agnosticism are too puny in scope and in dealing with ultimates to do more than to point to man's self-centered pride, while our own Christian traditional affirmation that this life settles eternity is of equally shriveled dimensions, based on immoral presuppositions at that. On the question of God's longer pedagogy and of life's stronger stretches for learning beyond our death we need to listen well and carefully to Hinduism and Buddhism.

The Christian faith can keep fresh and real as it tackles its new problems in creative faith. It must be free to scan every hope in God's world and to learn from all God's people. The focus of faith in Christ is the general direction of faith. Faith moves ever ahead in every age to face its distinctive problems. The focus provides no rigid doctrines that should occasion fixation of faith. Nor does it call for mere fugitiveness. Those who have been grasped once for all by the meaning of integrity and concern believe that they are themselves ultimates not only for man's search, but also for his finding. Not only are truth and love requisite for life and learning, but, also, faith discovers as it follows ever after them that they are dependable directions for moving toward the final goal. When Christ is the sign and symbol both for the search and for the finding, his life becomes for us the life, the truth, and the way into the ultimate dimensions of Spirit. Then God is no longer a premature final answer nor some vague, receding generality in any direction, but he becomes, rather, the focus which ever more fulfills even as it calls for ever-fuller seeking. The Christian faith provides truth as it is needed without ever doing away with the finality of faith.

III

No faith is real that does not suffer frustrations. All believers, if they are honest with themselves, know that they have trouble believing. Faith that does not stand in conflict with doubt is no faith. The deeper and fuller the faith, the stronger the doubt. Doubt is not only a matter of faith's need to grow and therefore of ever doubting its present attainment. All growing faith is doubting faith, doubt as to its present adequacy and doubt as to its right to move on toward the new loyalty. But the more far-reaching the direction of faith and the more daring its vision, the more the believer has scope and reason for doubt. Unless faith has strong doubts it is not strong faith. The faith that fulfills the most suffers the most severe frustrations.

But faith can sometimes suffer, not from conflict of faith

with doubt, but from lassitude. The believer's convictions can evaporate. Although he has never strongly doubted his faith, he has gradually listened approvingly to other faiths or begun to think differently about the ultimate meaning and direction of his life. After a while he no longer feels at all sure of his main faith, although none of the other faiths either can command his life. He seems not to know what he believes. Surely he does believe something, for obviously he goes on living and making choices in the light of some ultimates, but often his ultimates are divided and differ and he does not seem to have any one faith that grasps him and guides his life. He suffers from spiritlessness, from lack of meaning, from absence of purpose.

If our analysis has been right, faith can become frustrated by being turned into knowledge. The believer is led to expect, or concludes by himself, that he should believe what he sees. Seeing, he has heard, is believing. But seeing is precisely not believing. Therefore a man, pondering his knowledge of ultimates, may conclude that it can never be proved in any sense comparable to other knowledge. Or he may never weigh his faith thus coldly and consciously, but only know in his depth self that his faith cannot be proved. Or he may hear the constant challenge, both from true believers and from the enemies of his faith, that he really has no knowledge on which to base his faith. He may hear it scorned as arbitrary or unfounded.

For such frustration of faith there is no cure in terms of more knowledge. Any ultimates that can be known in terms of this life are not worthy of being believed to be such. Whatever can be described as foundational or satisfactory for faith in terms of human or historic experience can never be prescribed for faith. The fact is not only that no demonstrative evidence of a conclusive nature can be offered for faith; the further and decisive fact is that knowledge may not take the place of faith. Finite man must live by faith; man in time cannot put God's eternity under his control of knowledge. Therefore having a false expectation, he must always be frustrated.

The opposite side of the coin is for man to pitch his faith over against knowledge. He may conclude that since the more one knows the less one believes, the ideal state of faith is the assertion of the purely arbitrary or the completely absurd. Then after a while he finds himself believing for the sake of believing. He seeks faith not to find anything but faith. He believes not in any ultimate, but in faith for its own sake. But faith in faith is no faith, for faith moves ahead. Faith in faith may be faith in moving without moving anywhere. Such faith lacks focus or its focus is of no importance. Since no road can be known to lead anywhere, the logic goes, and yet faith should move, let us move anywhere at all. Then faith becomes mere movement for the sake of movement and not for the sake of finding any ultimate. Such faith is both fugitive and futile. Turned in on itself it may become aggressively hostile to knowledge, but within there is no convincing sense of movement, direction, or focus.

Thus faith is frustrated if turned into knowledge, and equally frustrated if turned away from knowledge. True faith lives by the focus of the direction toward which it is moving, even while knowing full well that it has not yet arrived. Faith should be power to test the spirits, to evaluate the facts, to weigh varying interpretations in the light of personal and general experience. It should do so in the light of the fullest facts available and the most critical as well as the most creative reason. In this way there will be no lurking uneasiness within to the effect that faith is rationalization of desire and not interpretation in the light of both truth and true need.

When faith is turned neither into knowledge nor into an excuse for not thinking, the believer is open to examine alternate faiths in order to learn from them within his own faith or even to choose among them. In such a case he does not substitute faith for study. He does not mistake creative speculation for critical examination. His faith, while moving ahead toward a goal, is never up in the air. It relates to life. It concerns needs. It is involved in the wholeness of knowledge, for faith must be frustrated without focus as well as frustrated when the focus for moving ahead in the search is mistaken for the goal itself.

There are also, similarly, frustrations of faith owing to feeling and to willing. Faith is man's total response to the call of God. Therefore, the suppression of any essential function of the self will result in the frustration of faith. In the next chapter we shall try to clarify these matters which concern the structure and dynamics of faith as we proceed to analyze the fulfillment of faith. The main trouble, however, seems to lie in the relation between faith as believing in accordance with knowledge as focus, and faith as believing beyond and in spite of knowledge in its movement ahead with direction and purpose.

4: The Fulfillment of Faith

Faith becomes fulfilled partly through its activities and partly through the state of the self in faith. Faith is the whole life walking an unprovable way. Faith is the entire person living his choices. Faith is the person's reaching out toward the world that can help and hurt him, the reaching beyond the concrete world of immediate experience for such meaning, purpose, and fulfillment as life can give. We are our faith. We do not so much have faith as we are had by it. Faith is more the gift for our response and from it, and our life is according to our faith. We do not so much fulfill faith as faith fulfills us. The fulfillment of faith is not the faithfulness of walking alone, although this is part of faith, but it is our total fulfillment by the faith we are as we walk. False faiths disappoint and wound us. Genuine faith searches us, makes demands of us, but also fulfills us. How does such fulfillment come about?

In our total makeup we live through three basic functions: mind, spirit, and will. Affections, or "feelings," accompany these aspects and the pressures of our emotions influence the choices of each one of us, but the initiating elements in each individual are these three. Let us discuss their relation to the fulfillment of faith.

I

The nature of the mind is to be restless. The basic function of the mind is to act as interpreter. Each person responds to a world of which he must be aware in order to identify what is there, to discriminate among the items in his experience, to evaluate them, to store his appraisal in memory for further use, and to organize his whole world of experience. By such response a person can and should direct his life with regard both to the maximum reality and worth and also with a view to his fullest possible satisfaction or fulfillment. The two aims, deepest down, go together. The mind, then, is an activity of the self in relating itself to the world and in directing its activity. Unless the mind is used as fully and as well as possible, the person can forfeit much possible good and encounter much needless evil.

Therefore the nature of the mind is to be restless, to probe, to weigh, to wonder. The self as mind must examine what it observes, test what it experiences, and sort out what is worthwhile from what is unimportant or harmful. Therefore each person in his mental activity needs to be ever alert, to leave no material unexamined, to weigh and classify all his experiences in order the most adequately to serve the self as will in the directing of its onward march of life.

At whatever point the mind is forbidden to probe any subject, precisely there it loses confidence in its own usefulness or in its being needed, and develops fears and frustrations in relation to the fenced-off area. The self as mind may find that others have wisely solved areas of experience; then it can seek and try these areas and find satisfaction in accepting the results and in using them in further search. The self as mind, through learning, makes the walking of past generations its own and continues the walking. Education thus leads not to frustration but to fulfillment of life.

But intellectual no-trespassing signs frustrate us and give us basic insecurities. When men are not allowed to interpret revelation for themselves on account of its absolute authority but must accept it as it is, the mind, by thus being fenced out and deprived of its rightful function, feels frustrated.

This restlessness of mind as part and parcel of its very nature and function precludes revelation as finished answers from above. We can now view from a specific perspective what the first chapter attempted to say concerning the inadequacies of biblicism, creedalism, and Catholicism. When the Bible becomes the source book of foundational significance for the Christian faith rather than the textbook with all the answers, when it becomes the accumulation of religious history under God and not the encyclopedia of all knowledge, then the Bible has become a central storehouse of our religious heritage. The Bible must minister to the rightful restlessness of the mind not by giving final answers but by indicating only general directions for faith.

Such also is the case with creedalism and Catholicism. As confessions of faith, not as statements of fact, the creeds can indicate the substance of the church's witness. As such they can give way to fuller and better statements of creative faith, baptized in the critical spirit of our age. The restless mind must continuously be reworking the whole of the Christian faith with reference to man's ever-new knowledge. Catholicism, similarly, can be the continuing home of faith only when it will allow its children room to mature. It must set them free not only to accept or reject the faith, but personally to keep rethinking and applying it. It must allow more opportunity for laymen to participate in the formulation and the application of the faith. Catholicism should be the teaching home of the needy children of men, the mother who cares and who shares her best knowledge as well as her best life.

The restless mind is not like a horse fed on oats, "r'aring to go," that has to have exercise for the sake of exercise. The mind does not feel satisfied with work for the sake of work. The mind wants to pull the wagon or run the race. The self as mind feels frustrated both when it is fenced out from certain areas of thought and when it is made to perform meaningless labor. The mind exists for the purpose of finding truth and needs to accumulate its findings, not merely always to seek and never to find. Theologically, this means that the restless mind, with us, craves to examine its heritage and heritages in order to participate in the creation of the present history of faith, particularly by relating heritage to hope, and hope to heritage.

With our heritage of Christianity today not only in basic

disrepute among countless thinking people outside the church but also under radical and often destructive reformulation within its own ranks, with it threatened, in fact, by a modernity empty of meaning and power for life, the so-called Christian faith can be seen to have failed the world in its drift toward both inner and outer destruction. Only when intellectually competent persons of faith can be free with regard to both our faith's total heritage and all other hopes, and thus engage in an age of constructive study, can we begin to acquire the kind of unity of direction for life and civilization which our age demands.

The mind needs a pattern that is both open and yet directive. It needs a focus that is as dependable as destiny, and that yet lacks specific directions. The work of interpretation must neither be done already nor be without decisive meaning. Such a pattern, such a focus of interpretation is Christ as the life of God for man. The kind of love that came in Jesus, *agape*, provides the mind all the faithfulness of God for meaning and yet also offers the ever-creative newness of concrete experience as a meaningful task.

The person as interpreter can confront Christian doctrines and see how alien philosophies have made them false. We are just beginning to understand that we cannot borrow the framework of faith without thereby distorting it. The holy love of God in Christ is a kind of life that can be used as the basis of both meaning and motivation, never in a static or fixed sense, but always in a dynamic and creative manner. Theology can be no closed, self-consistent system. It can be no more than the provision of ever-new directives for faith in life from within the living experience of walking with God.

Generations of strong thinkers are needed to make the basic transition to such a theology within a consistent Christian framework; and even then the task will need ever-fresh redoing.

Similarly, there is no Christian ethics as a set of fixed rules for conduct. This field needs the restless mind in a peculiar degree. But there is, nevertheless, a dependable pattern for Christian living. When Christ's love motivates man, creative concern is generated, but never along the lines of absolute principles. Such concern labors to understand creatively both in terms of the ever-variable concrete situation and also of such general rules as spring from the structures of a community of concern. *Agape* alone is final, but that finality is as open and new as life itself. *Agape* is as creative as the God who gives it. Thus the mind finds satisfaction in the service of a flexible faith. *Agape* is indispensable to life and yet not merely or mostly a matter of rules and regulations that can be given to man directly.

In the same way, those who must relate the Christian faith to the thoughts and practices of the secular world have no ready-made answers, but they do have a general focus. They have a pole of living truth that provides a steady perspective without supplying the vision that comes only as we walk toward our work. Some think that the Christian has a right to tell the world what to do; others are of the opinion that all the Christian can do is to ask relevant questions. Neither side is right. There is a Christian stance for conduct, or definite directives in general, but the faith never tells how the many existential principles of the faith can be used together or with regard to other ways of walking. Thus there is constant work for the mind, albeit within a security of being grasped by a truth that beckons commandingly from afar.

Once again, the steady directive yet flexible instruction of *agape*, or outgoing concern, makes it possible for the restless mind to carry on meaningful conversation with those who hold faiths other than the Christian. Nothing less than *agape* will do for either faith or life. God's faithfulness for man and man's concern for his fellow man in integrity of acceptance and co-operation are basic conditions for religion as such. This is, of course, the heart of the Christian faith, but this truth is as universal as human need. Nevertheless the faithfulness of God and the concern of man do not come prefabricated into history but must be worked out according to their general pattern. Therefore the interpreter can be fully hospitable to all non-Christian hopes for history while yet having as a definite nonrestrictive directive that whatever falls short of this depth-meaning of faith will have to be discarded, corrected, or fulfilled. The restless mind insists, within such an understanding, that no religion is to be accepted or rejected as such, but that all religions, including the Christian, need to be confronted with the revolutionary creativity of God's *agape*. Thus with regard to other religions a person can both satisfy the proper restlessness of his mind and yet also know the deep fulfillment of having a definite focus in general for his encounter of faith.

In this way the person in his rightful functioning as restless mind can be fulfilled both in the not seeing and in the seeing, both in the seeking and in the finding. Fulfillment of faith is to be had not as attained knowledge, but only as the

ever-dynamic moving toward that light that in this life we
shall never fully see.

II

Restless though the self as mind must remain in order to
become fulfilled, the self as spirit must ever rest in faith.
(For convenience and brevity we shall use in the ensuing
discussion "mind" and "spirit" instead of the more accurate
"self as mind" and "self as spirit.") Faith is anticipated attainment at its heart. Faith is reaching into reality or being
reached by it at its center far below every understanding of
the experience. The head and hand may be busy but the
heart must be at rest in God.

Faith finds God and enables the spirit to rest in him even
while the mind keeps working in both doubt and seeing, in
both mystery and meaning. Faith in its inmost reality is not
intellectual nor is it an activity. Faith is a state of the spirit,
a relationship to the spiritual world.

What then is spirit? Spirit is the image of God in man.
Spirit is man's capacity for God. God made man for himself
and man is restless until he rests in God. There is no other
rest for man. The mind within and the world without drive
restlessly on through ever-new changes. There is no halting
the process without fixation and frustration. But the man of
faith avoids fugitive shifting by letting himself be grasped
and fulfilled by God even while he knows that he has not
yet attained, but must ever press on toward the goal which is
only dimly and generally seen as a kind of life.

The spirit of man is created spirit. It never becomes nor

can become God. But it can make room for God within its life. It can become fulfillingly related to God. The fulfilled spirit knows the joy of resting in God in the midst of trouble, of struggling, of suffering, and even of defeat and death. Such resting cannot be touched by this world, for it is not of this world. Spiritual rest always transcends this world in its very midst. Accepting this world, it is more than conqueror within its seeming defeat; the spirit knows rest in the turmoil of restlessness; it knows fulfillment in the heart of frustration.

Such fulfillment of the spirit comes in three different manners. The first is the fulfillment of nature as man matures in right relation to God. By opening up to God's presence beyond understanding, and beyond even personal power of will, man finds that the strange haunting within him, although he still continues to think and act, is nevertheless stilled by a peculiar power that grasps him as he reaches out for it. He knows a deep inner peace. Satisfaction settles over the hubbub and he knows the healing touch of eternity on his life.

There is no substitute for personal experience in this realm of the spirit. No one can take the place of anyone else as he stands before God. Spirit rests only in God through worship. Man must learn to worship by himself. There is no substitute for prayer. Some dismiss prayer as mysticism. Some scorn it as pietism. But no religious experience can become personal in any dimension of depth that does not center in the genuineness of intercourse with the Eternal through prayer.

Prayer can, of course, be escape, and all too often it is.

In Little Rock, interviewing sociologists pointed out, during the hottest fight over the admission of Negro students to Central High School some of the local ministers who did nothing, and in fact did not even take an effective stand, felt holy relief about the situation because they had called a meeting to pray about it. Such prayers!

Or, to consider the matter not only socially but individually, once at an opening retreat of a theological seminary some participants were highly critical of there having been no opening prayer, and, as a matter of fact, no worship at all during the whole first afternoon. Later pondering on the occasion, however, one critic recalled that the actual opening had been an invitation for the whole school community to donate much-needed blood. What a symbol! What guilty feelings for the critic who in fact had never given his own while the small school gave one hundred pints. Even a doctor's orders not to give could not down a feeling that perhaps the opening of school with a call to bloodgiving might have been more appropriate than the most beautiful prayer, however sincere.

Jesus in the Sermon on the Mount puts the order thus: "Whoever does and teaches." Perhaps at times we should say, "Whoever does the right and prays." The Bible says the prayers of a righteous man have power. But the abuse of prayer should not stop us from the right use of it. Prayer is indispensable to the spirit's resting, deeply resting in God.

All religions cultivate prayer. Prayer is the native breath of the spirit. Through prayer and through prayer alone do men learn to know God personally and to feed the spiritual life. Prayer is communion of spirit with Spirit. Some have difficulty with the personal nature of prayer. Prayer pre-supposes an I-thou relationship. But prayer need not pre-suppose God as an enclosed individual of our human type of personality.

God who is personal Spirit, the Spirit who is love, far transcends any idea we have of personality in his inclusive relation to all there is. And yet we can believe beyond our understanding that such Spirit is structured and centered in truth and concern. We can believe that the Spirit who is Love understands and answers the deepest need of the free spirit to become himself, that is to identify himself with his truest nature, with God's inclusive integrity and concern in himself and for the world. There are resources for spirit in God, through prayer, that can astonish not only the world but any human being, whoever he is.

What full faith in God for the world can accomplish is only hinted at by the great lives of prayer and concern who have moved the world. The challenge of Spirit on spirit for the fulfillment not only of personality but of the whole creation is ever open. Faith rests in the fulfillment of nature within man's right relation to God. Participating in spirit in God's life for the world, man finds the most complete ful-fillment toward the future by resting already in God. Through unity of spirit with other men his little spirit is stretched within the illimitable power of the grace of God. Faith finds rest only as it rests in grace. Its sufficiency is never of itself, but of God.

Faith rests also, moreover, within that state of acceptance which is forgiveness. Man is, first of all, God's creature and as such needs fulfillment of nature. But he is also sinner. He puts his own concerns before those of God and others. He "curves in on himself." He becomes estranged and alienated both from himself and from his world. Fearing the One who loves him unconditionally, he flees and fights God. As sinner, he develops guilt feelings which separate him from God, take his mind in bondage, and pervert the truth. Guilt feelings paralyze his hands from doing genuine good, freeing them to do only such good as seems to promote or protect the self. They keep the feelings of satisfaction from flowing.

Thus man loses his convictions. They seem to evaporate, he knows not how or why. At the same time his whole self is restless. He uses his mind to defend his ever more ingenious rationalizations. He grows devious, hiding even from himself in self-justifications. He shuns the prophets of truth and right, while listening avidly to all who glorify man's revolt against God. He spurns the reformers as those who stir up trouble, who cannot let the sleeping dogs of his conscience lie.

There is no do-it-yourself cure for sin. Man must face the ultimate and be convicted, through and through, of his inability to lead a satisfactory life apart from his right relation to reality, to God the righteous as well as the merciful, to his judge as well as his savior. Only a repentance that goes to the very depths of the sinful will and only full acceptance of God's inclusive will for the world can ever fully relieve man of his guilt and give him rest. The sinner flees, says the Bible, and no man pursues him. The guilty spirit cannot rest. If man's spirit is to rest, he must find forgiveness and remaking.

Some theologians claim that we can know ourselves accepted even though unacceptable. This is a great half truth.

We can know God who accepts all in whatever condition because he loves all unconditionally. We can also trust that his acceptance is constant for all, since even "if we are faithless, he remains faithful—for he cannot deny himself." But our acceptance by God involves nevertheless our willingness to be accepted on his terms only. We may not have the strength even to want to accept his terms of righteousness, let alone have any idea that we can fulfill them, but we must be willing both to want to want and to trust God's grace beyond our capacity to believe, that by his power he can make us acceptable and keep us acceptable in his sight, not as perfected people but as those determined, by his grace, to keep walking in the fullest way of faith and life. In such a state of forgiveness the spirit finds rest. Thus to be accepted by God is to find in the now the fulfillment of faith.

Not only can the spirit rest in God with respect to its newly fulfilled nature and with respect to its state of forgiveness, but even the restless mind can find a deeper rest in the spirit. Such can be the case since the self of the spirit, even while the mind is constantly at work seeking and never finding final answers, can yet profoundly experience the truth that the total person can rest even while the mind, its servant, is restless. He can feel the reality of the presence of the Goal even while the mind is in hot pursuit of it.

Both the Catholic Church and the Reformers put the emphasis on the forgiveness of sin, the former through the juridical perspective and sacramental grace, the latter through justification by grace and faith alone; but in our day interpreters of faith like Paul Tillich are putting justification of the intellect by faith into the limelight as well. The mind, too, can rest, not as a function, or activity, but as justified already within God's revelation of himself, however much of search such revelation may then involve. Barth, too, stresses the centrality of the revelatory aspect of God's relation to man, justifying man's mind through grace. Revelation means God's self-revelation once for all in Jesus Christ, he says, and in this fullest sense there can be no other revelation. Although such revelation must in the nature of the case be wholly the work of God, man's mind is justified by grace far beyond his appropriation of this revelation.

With the coming of our new nature, the restless mind has a new master. The mind is part of a new being. When the spirit is forgiven and rightly related to Spirit, then the distorting pressures on the mind of self-justification are lifted. The forgiven man needs no self-justification. He is justified by God. "Who can be against him?" Then the mind can work on, ever seeking, and yet also finding beyond seeking. Such search is then no longer frantic; it is no longer the work of the oppressed self; it is no longer the seeking for refuge of the guilt-driven self.

Then even our doubts can contribute to the work of faith. By doubting the mind comes to know that it can never attain self-security through knowledge. It seeks for no hiding place from God through its own constructions. It need not bolster up its insecure ego nor blow up its proud self. Humbly man learns through the doubts that plague him that he must be justified by faith even in mind. Doubting then becomes not only the necessary counterpart of growth whereby the unserviceable old position becomes outmoded, but also the inevitable accompaniment of created man's reception of God's gracious work in revelation.

Thus the man of faith should be primarily at rest. There should be no reason why the Christian should not, at his deepest dimension, be as serene as the Buddhist ideal, which characterizes so much of Oriental art and life that after living with it intimately for a time, one begins to feel Western activism lacks religious depth. The early Christian church spoke of joy in the faith and of the victory of faith that overcomes the world. It accepted the renewing of the mind as well as the transformation of nature far beyond the mere forgiveness of sin.

It is, indeed, necessary to know the distance between God and man, in such a measure and in such a manner that we know we can never know it. We must see how sinful man falls forever short of the grace of God, but even more and in a deeper dimension still, we must all understand that forgiveness is for the sake of the new being, for the new nature in the new relation, and that within this relation there is rest. There is no mere passivity or lassitude in that rest, but a joy and peace which surpass understanding. No religion is real and rightly related to God that at its deepest state of finding does not offer such "a joy and peace in believing."

III

Alongside the restless self as mind and the self at rest as spirit is the ruling self as will. Man's deepest relation to God, Emil Brunner has kept urging, is as a responsible being. Even when man turns away from God he is responsible, his very suffering and efforts at self-justification bearing witness to this fact. Because man is created responsibly free, man can regulate his relation to God. Such power does not pre-suppose that man can create the relation. No man can build a bridge to God. But God never forces man to cross the bridge he builds for him. God never drags man across unwillingly to a relationship of love and communion. Even man's obedience, in order to be real, must be from the heart; it must be willed by man. All is of grace. All depends on faith. But both grace and faith include within their gifts the reality of responsible freedom. Therefore even though all is of God, except man's abuse of his freedom, nevertheless man is given a ruling will to regulate his relation to God, to the world, and to himself.

Thus the will can command the mind. The will is responsible for the direction of the search. Man can set the compass of his search toward God. He can will to pursue ultimate concern. He can decide on integrity of examination. He can turn himself pro-universe rather than contra-universe. He can take the side of what William James called the "will to believe." How a man wills to face the world and in what attitude makes a basic difference to what he finds. Unless he at least seeks the main road he surely cannot find it.

The self as ruling will can thus be determined to keep on going in the direction of truth. It can decide for concerned truth rather than rebellious or indifferent truth. The true rebellion is the revolt against all sham. It is the repudiation of hypocrisy. It is the scorning of the broad way of easy conformity. It is the seeing through and rejecting the smooth pose of a nonconformity which is, in fact, the proper selective conformity. It can dare to break down the justifications that keep the community from facing the truth, as thus bringing down upon itself the wrath of the community. It can regulate its search toward the creative finding of the truth that matters. The indifferent truth is not worth the sharing. Truth for truth's sake is an empty formality. Such truth need not be communicated. Only truth for the sake of life, in the service of life, counts in the truest scale. There never was an age, I believe, that needed positive, creative, constructive, concerned thinking more than today. History is in the balance. It cannot be saved by heritage. It must find the fuller hope to fulfill its heritage and all the heritages of men as men.

The ruling will must be careful, however, not to disregard the right to believe. The will to believe cannot create truth ultimately. Neither reality nor salvation is of man's making. Therefore the will, like the mind, must finally find rest in the spirit. The self as will can easily try to become its own lord and to create its own love. But Lordship and Love belong to God, who gives them to us through the Spirit.

The ruling will must not heed the cost nor dread the effort, but must redirect its creative power to its proper task in the right direction. If the road signs are obscure and the person seems lost, the ruling will must bid the mind to keep going even without signs. Faith never teaches fulfillment along a road easy or well marked all the way. Faith cannot depend on merely external guides. The man of faith must be a man of ruling will who commands the restless mind to work on in the set direction; and even in the dark, when move it must, it gropes its way as best it can, until the light breaks once again upon some path ahead.

So it is with the affections. The ruling will must listen to their reports of past experience. Not to hear the report of the feelings is to disregard the fount of experience. In our feelings we often reach dimensions of depth far below mere intellectual seeing. The more spiritual our nature, the more sensitive and deep-reaching the affections in our life.

But to heed the feelings by themselves is to court disaster in the life of faith. The feelings are partial to immediate satisfaction. They crave fullness of expression. Often there have to be choices of truth where the feelings object out of anxiety and dread. They seem to pre-feel the hurt. They seem to feel in advance the cost of the decision. They urge us to take the safety of the familiar path or advise slow motion. The conscientious feelings urge us to enjoy our heritage rather than to create adventuresome history. The ruling will must often act contrary to the person's emotions. He may not feel like taking a certain action, but he knows that he must, in order to be truthful and concerned.

But the feelings deceive us. After the feelings have had their immediate gratification at the expense of the total self, the fuller self rebels and brings its own feelings of guilt, regret, and mortification into play. Then the self suffers and knows through the feelings themselves that they cannot be depended upon as guides to set the direction or the pace of faith. Faith must be fulfilled by the affection of the total self. Indeed, man must become fulfilled also through the emotions which accompany the potential self. Present gratification should not stand in the way of eventual attainment. The ruling will can choose one or the other, or be torn, and even torn asunder, between them.

At the cost of present enjoyment, as it seems, the ruling will can command the march of faith in line with duty and concern. It can determine to forego satisfaction for the sake of truth. It can bear its cross with patience in choosing God's will to the best of its knowledge. And observe! The feelings do find satisfaction! Some of us have known life's most dread decisions. We have had to choose between approval and abuse. We have had to choose between acceptance and honor, on the one hand, and rejection and infamy on the other. How desperately we have wanted such a cup of decision to pass from us. We have not sought for such alternatives! At least we had not been conscious of where our choices were leading us until the time of crisis came upon us. How we dreaded keeping on! How we longed to turn around for approval, perhaps even for fame and profit. But by God's grace, ambivalent and ambiguous though the choices may have been, and foolish though some manners of our pursuing the road have seemed, nevertheless upon making the dread choice of truth and right as best we knew, we have found the peace of God's approval and inner rest as never before. The angels of approving feelings always minister to God's chosen as they emerge victoriously from their Gethsemane struggles.

Such is the testimony of faith; such is the witness of experience. The emotions of a restless struggling self can never come to full rest. To think they can is to fail to understand the life we must lead in this world as creatures in the process of growth as well as finite beings in the valley of decision. But the ruling will can teach us that the fullest satisfactions, even of the feelings, come with the fulfillment of the total self as it moves in the direction of the deepest truth and right it knows, at the fullest speed.

Even the emotions can thus find the transcendent release, beyond relief, of the spirit's rest. There are feelings not of this world. Ecstasy is the exceptional moment when we are lifted into harmony with the unconditional. Such emotions there are, indescribable to all and hintable only to those who have known them in experience. But there are also the steady affections that accompany the self as spirit. These are the affections of the new being. They can become so real and so connected with the ruling will, as it keeps directing the self in its way to God, that although the other emotions come and go, disrupting and distracting, even quite upsetting and humiliating the self, nevertheless these affections of the new being provide more and more the steady balance wheel of life.

The ruling will meets less and less resistance. The self as spirit becomes more and more central to the habitual response of life. Then man knows, even in this life, something of what the Bible calls the experience of being blessed. He discovers the fulfillment of faith which does not mean the end of seeking or of struggling, but involves a fulfillment of spirit, a dimension of depth, a transcendence of ordinary experience that go far below, beyond, and above happiness or sorrow. Then man finds the fulfillment of faith as the total self, fulfilled even in feeling, rests for time and eternity in God.

The ruling will, moreover, must finally itself be satisfied. There can be no fulfilled faith without a life of true righteous-ness. We wince at such words. We shun them as belonging to a narrow and life-repressing faith, all too often touched with fanaticism. But we must come back to them, not merely as words but as reality. Without righteousness there can be no vital, no convincing, no commanding faith.

Righteousness means a life where the ruling will intends the right and works to implement its decision. Righteousness means wholeness of life. Righteousness means genuineness of life. It means being real, being authentic. The ruling will must be in the service of the total self, as spirit rightly related to God through faith, in integrity and in concern. Such relation is righteousness. Without such relation faith cannot fulfill man. The more such relation is steadily attained and retained, the more faith can grow.

We are afraid of righteousness because it smacks of "moralism." The one thing we must not be is moralistic. To be moralistic is to be holier than thou. To be moralistic is to be conscious of one's being "good," and perhaps better than most. To be moralistic stands for being critical of other people. Moralism stands for a small-scaled standard of not violating more or less minor taboos: not dancing, not smoking, not drinking, not swearing, not cheating, not telling dirty stories, or in some circles, not even going to the movies or playing cards. Moralism stands for going to church or chapel, to revival meetings and prayer meetings, being saved within the conformist respectability of one's own little ingroup.

Moralism means technically prestation, paying a debt. It means a work which we offer to God in order to be right with him. This work takes the place of our being accepted by God as we are because he loves us, and of the opening of our lives to his great concern for others, resting in him in sheer faith and gratitude. Multitudes work away at being right with God. Such work gets in God's way. They feel ever more guilty and critical of others. They lose the juices of life and dry up in their moralism. They feel superior to others, even while they are the most lost. Jesus classified such "good" people, such respectable people, as worse than the worst; they were further from God than any sinner who knew that he was one.

Thus today we hate moralism and despise the pious. All of this religiosity seems sham, humbug. We are even getting conscious that doing good, both personally and socially, also can be a matter of moralism, of seeking self-security and self-righteousness. Therefore we have come to scorn the "do-gooder," suspecting his motives and despising the results, for such do-gooding makes him feel superior and humiliates the receiver at his deepest. Therefore we revolt against every form of charity, and may question and even dismiss all causes. We want to be real, we say. We cannot even be genuine ourselves; why should we export our lack of righteousness, our own insecurity, our own attempt at being right, at the expense of a crooked world? The world is bent enough as it is.

Few writers have more sharply deflated idealism than Albert Camus. Jean Baptiste Clamence, the narrating character of *The Fall*, helped a blind man across the street. When they had crossed over, the blind man lifted his hat in appreciation, whereupon Clamence lifted his in return only to recognize the fact that since he was aware that the blind man could not see his courteous gesture, he had really done it in order to gain the plaudits of the passersby. He knew full well, he thought to himself, that he had helped the man cross the street not because he cared for him but because he wanted the approval of the crowd and his own approval of himself as judged by the crowd.

Feeling like this man, we too suspect our motives for doing good and think ourselves genuine when we inhibit our inclination to help, recognizing instead our "true" nature. But such reasoning is really the accepting of our lower self as the real self. In fact, it is sophisticated rationalization of inaction. This kind of thinking, too, can be and usually is escape!

When we thus reason with ourselves, however, we usually fail to see that now we are glorifying failure as genuine. We are calling the lack of fulfillment an authentic state of all men. If we confess such failure we think we are somehow right and acceptable. But here is the mischief! True, such honesty is good and needed; but to glory in it, to make it a norm, is not only to kill moral incentive but, indeed, is itself the real moralism. This standard is but another way of saying that we can be right with God by merely admitting that we are wrong, or perhaps that we can be right without any ultimates. All we have done, of course, is to make a god in our own worse image and called others to worship it. Whoever does not fall down before it we cast into the burning oven of unacceptability, of isolation, or of abuse.

Our need, instead, is the humility that knows its complete dependence upon God, that never mistakes its own attainment for God's measure of right and wrong, that never dares to stand above others to judge them, but that, seeking the way of integrity and concern, commits itself wholly to them, trusting only God's grace while accepting continual forgiveness and correction. This is the righteousness of the ruling will that comes from obedience within the community of faith.

Such standards are the heart of the New Testament: love fulfills the whole law, but love comes only from God in the Spirit. The Spirit who comes to direct and help us within the free community of trust is, indeed, the Holy Spirit. He comes in righteousness, not of external deeds that can be learned, but of intention and of judgment, of study and of implementation. Such conduct is existential and contextual, that is, it is a matter of personal deeds of obedience within the context of faith's community of concern. Without such existential commitment and without such a community of concern faith cannot find fulfillment.

We need, in fact, a new kind of puritanism, not the puritanism of moralism, not the puritanism that kills pleasure and shrinks from fullness of life, not the puritanism of rigid mores and cramping customs, but the puritanism of holy obedience in humble faith and concern. Such puritanism will release creative seeing and constructive civilization. Such puritanism will usher in the co-operative era. Such puritanism will find community directives that will not stultify life by being imposed upon it, but be offered for life's needed discipline.

Such puritanism will not neglect the social, the political, the economic, and the international relations for personal responsibilities. It will search out our collective guilt and face our common straying from the right. Such puritanism, for instance, will accept the inclusiveness of creative race relations without causism. It will trust in no "ism" for salvation. It will blame no social category for our sinfulness as men. It will dare, rather, in faith to be judged by God, to search out our failures, and to direct our feet into the paths of peace. No modern righteousness can be mostly personal. All ethical questions today demand that their social dimension be fully included.

Nor can such righteousness leave out the total redoing of the life of the church through the restless mind and the obedient will. The church as an institution must be thoroughly searched out, weighed in the balance, pronounced both guilty and innocent, and be radically remade in the full image of the inclusive and concerned community of the Christ of God. Jesus will no longer be misused as an idol, worshiped in the place of God, but restored to God's way, truth, and life for man.

In one sense of stress at least those are right, no matter how much scoffed at they may be today, who held and hold that Paul changed the Gospel of Jesus. Jesus stressed as of primary importance the fact that we are according to our faith, that "according to our faith it shall be done unto us," that we must first of all make the tree good, that we can then judge men not according to the faith they confess but according to the faith they live. If justification by faith, as it is sometimes presented à la St. Paul, shortchanges this truth of Jesus, we have surely lost a primary element of God's truth for the world.

The truth is that faith can reach fulfillment even now as it rests in God. Each person can be fulfilled as spirit. But such fulfillment of spirit makes right use of the restless mind and of the ruling will. Fulfillment comes only with mental search and righteous living. The finality of faith, then, is not faith as such. We believe not so much in faith as in God. The man of faith rests in God, thinks in God, and works in God. The finality of faith is real for our finding, for our participation in God's life; for when we truly discover the faith, we know that what we have found is that we can both be found by and fulfilled by God. Such faith is final. It secures the highest fulfillment life affords.

PART II

CHRISTIANITY

AMONG THE

WORLD RELIGIONS

5: Christianity and World Faith

Do you suppose God is the God of the Jews alone? Is he not the God of Gentiles also? Certainly, of Gentiles also, if it be true that God is one. Romans 3:29-30 (New English Bible).

If the world survives and unless civilization is set back beyond present imagination, we Christians shall have to decide what attitude we are going to take toward the world's religions. This decision is now inescapable and there are four major choices.

The first choice, which seems obvious, is that the Christian faith alone is true and that all other religions are pagan and false. I reject this answer on two grounds: it is unbiblical and must be rejected from within the faith itself. Paul has given us the final, definitive answer: If it be true that God is one, then all who worship him must in some way worship the one God. My second reason for rejecting this answer is that it

[87

makes Christianity esoteric; that is, it makes it a private and partial affair. If God is creator of all the ends of the earth, religion is essential to all and is God's call in all people. The religions of the world then spring necessarily as a response to God's call to all people. As man's need for God, religion is the deepest drive of human nature. There can no more be a Hindu, a Christian, or a Baha'i medicine of immortality than there can be a Chinese, Aryan, or Indian cure for cancer.

The second answer to the relation between the Christian faith and the religions of the world is that there is a common center of truth deep within all religions, although all religions of course come in relative form. I reject this highly inviting answer also, on two grounds. First, it is too intellectualistic without sufficient awareness of the concrete nature of the religions themselves. Whatever method we use to ascertain the common truth we can never find it, for religion is not basically a matter of reason. God is not mind, and religion is no system of reason. I am not merely denying that all religious normativeness or standard is rational in nature; I am affirming that basically religion is not a matter of truth but a matter of life. This position of a common center of truth contained deep within all religions, beneath their relative form, also fails to understand that man's sinfulness makes such a center impossible. Man fights and flees God. Yes, man even hates God, perhaps especially within his religions, and therefore the deeper centers of the religions do not coincide and in their coinciding point to God. Religion is man's response in sin and fear as well, and therefore the religions keep diverging; they do not necessarily converge and point to one God.

A third answer to the relation between the Christian faith

and the religions of the world is to the effect that all religions are relative and, coming out of their own culture, each religion is best for its own people. I reject that also—and confidently—on two grounds. Such relativism, which we usually call pluralism, denies in the first place the *essential* nature of religion. It is better, I believe, than calling just one religion true, because at least this position universalizes relativity. I am going to suggest, in the second place, that there is a common center, not *in* the religions, but *for* the religions.

One form of religious pluralism is Hinduism's claim to be the universal religion, because it is inclusive of all the religions. Paul Tillich calls Christianity ultimate because Christianity refuses, he says, to make itself ultimate. In the cross, Dr. Tillich affirms, Christianity dies to its sinful pretension to ultimacy and rises in this death to the true ultimacy, the knowing that no religion is ultimate. But, analytically, both these claims to ultimacy conceal behind a positive verbal façade their implicit espousal of relativism.

Hinduism and Tillich are, in fact, guilty of what I am beginning to call the "illicit infinite." They claim that the infinite cannot be defined by a relative or in relation to the finite, without becoming limited by it. But the infinite that does not include and thoroughly interpenetrate the finite that we do know, is not infinite! Certainly it cannot be infinite if it does not include, and relate itself positively to, the being that we now know; and therefore we know that they are operating with an illicit infinite. This illicit infinite leads to the great negation that God cannot be reliably known; and this great negation leads to the great refusal to try to find out how he is known.

The fourth answer—to which I subscribe—is that there

once was a concrete life that at its center conclusively suggested in life and teaching the universal love of God; that this life of outgoing, inclusive, unconditional concern, engendering an open community of creative concern, is normative *for* all religions. I believe that this life, Jesus as the Christ, is normative for *all* religions. This concrete center, not *in* the religions but *for* all religions, at the same time rejects the concrete formulations and actual behavior of all religions and also accepts them for revision and fulfillment, both in reorientation and in remotivation at their own deepest potential.

In other words, what is *truest* in the religions is not *central* either to their thinking or to their living. The fact that Christ is not *in* but *for* all religions demands a radical reappraisal and retooling of all religions.

Judaism, in love to God and neighbor, feels for God's universal love at its deepest potential; but Judaism has always rejected this answer by actual nationalistic, cultural, and religious in-groupism. While accepting its own religious and cultural past, Judaism can turn itself inside out by accepting its own true potential: who Christ was and what Christ really taught.

What about Christianity? Christianity has at times and in good part stood in life and thought for its own normative event: God's love in Christ. Christianity occasionally has paid full attention to Jesus Christ—but only occasionally. For its entire structure of doctrine has denied its Lord by its eternal dualism of heaven and hell, which is a complete contradiction of the living ultimacy of Christ as love. In life, Christianity has steadily rejected the Christ by sanctifying the status quo—in nationalism, in race relations, in all the ways of the world.

Buddhism, while it does not make universal love ultimate to doctrine or practice, does witness to God's call by its refusal to take ordinary experience as standard for religion, by its keen sense of evil, by its central legend that the Buddha, instead of accepting his own deliverance, was willing to renounce it in order to save the people, and also by its dwelling on compassion both in thought and in life. Buddhism can realize its own true potential by accepting love as its center in place of its actual center, by becoming a universal community of concern open to eternal compassion. It may be easier for Buddhists and Hindus to accept Christ than for us Christians. It may be. We may too long have neglected what Christ means.

I am convinced that the universal love of God, in a quality of life and within a community of concern, can awaken in the world the creative, co-operative spirit. In this spirit we can solve our common problems as men together. I believe that in this universal love we can be lifted to the power of mutual acceptance that shall help thaw out the wintry banks of religious indifference, impotence, and antagonism, and let the growth of spring give new promises to a world of creation wherein men can be more challenged by the opportunities than weighed down by all the dangers and all the problems.

I believe that there is hope for the world, if we genuinely accept the full meaning of who Christ was—the universal love of God, whom we can completely accept and completely trust. I believe with all my heart that we can have a new day, as people, as churches, as a world, when we begin—instead of merely using this universal love for our own self-protection and self-promotion—to cut loose and apply it in all the relationships of life, insofar as we start with ourselves, with the family, with our churches, but go on to the ends of the world with the whole gospel. We must accept the reality of him who once in human history was so thoroughly imbued with the presence of God that we know what reality is and how we can live it.

Do you suppose God is the God of the Christians alone? Is he not the God of the non-Christians also? Certainly, of the non-Christians also, if it be true that God is one.

6: The Universal Dimensions of the Christian Faith

Everywhere we hear that a new world needs a new faith. The Christian faith accordingly is being drastically revised to fit a new age. Not surprisingly, this wave of revaluation rocks the boat of the missionary enterprise. The finality of the Christian faith certainly belongs to no particular formulation of it, but only to its inherent nature. Christians all over the world, without self-justification or in-group psychology, need to understand the universal nature of our faith and to reformulate our missionary message accordingly.

The Christian faith centers in the universal, unconditional love of God. Christ as the Son of God communicates the fact that God who is sovereign, holy love has entered into a concrete human life, Jesus of Nazareth, to show us his nature and to offer us his presence and his power. The sovereign Lord is saving Love.

From this central act of revelation follow with full and natural consequence three basic truths for all men: a universal God, a universal community, and a universal man. Christian world mission is merely the acceptance of the mandate of its own nature.

The universal God has ever tried and everywhere keeps trying to reveal himself to man's free response. There has never been nor can there ever be limited access to the universal God of unconditional concern. The universal priesthood of believers expresses the fundamental fact that the Christian Way is no superhighway with limited access.

The only way to God is the open highroad of following, in life and thought, whatever truth is available to any people and to any man. God is the spirit of truth, for perfect love casts out not only fear but all that is false. Christ as the fullest combination of the summary and the symbol of the God who is Love is the only way to the Father precisely because in him God declares as false any way that is loveless and untrue.

Concretely Christ means, then, that we Christians, to live our faith, must be willing to understand all faiths and all peoples, in their own religious commitments, to converse with them with full respect, and to work with them and for them in concerned co-operation. If our joint aim for concerned truth is genuine, we can trust God for the results. I have been astonished in discussions with non-Christians throughout the world to learn how ready they are for any Christian insights that stand the test of open communication.

The God who is universal, unconditional love calls for an open, inclusive community. Christianity is inherently normative sociology. Such a universal God calls for a creative and concerned community. He wills that we cleanse and rework our theology in line with his self-declared nature. The community may do no less if it is to have integrity, for our actual Christian theology is mixed with immoral and unintelligent doctrines that fall abysmally short of God's revelation in Christ.

The universal community is the purpose for which God created the world. All societal relations find standard, direction, and creative power with respect to God's inclusive will for all and each. Our communities fail when they fall short of cultivating the freedom and faithfulness in fellowship that spring out of creative concern. The true Christian church transcends within its own self-being racial discrimination, national divisiveness, social caste-ism, as well as all other separations, large or small, that are caused by ill will, greed, lust for power, particularly when these appear in the guise of partial loyalties and historic obligations. Instead, God's will for co-operative living, beyond necessary competitive stimulus, provides the power for human freedom to decide for, and to struggle into, the good community of grace which is ever the free gift of God.

Nowadays it is fashionable to castigate the church. It is even considered proper for church leaders to cast religion out of the church. Be it admitted that the church all over the world, as my recent trip has made clear to me, is a travesty of the universal community in Christ which is its very nature. Be it clear that religiosity is the lowest form of sham. Nevertheless two things remain: the true community is ours for the accepting, and it is available in proportion to our trusting the universal God and entering the universal Way of Christ.

Frail and sinful human beings, we shall fall short, but God's grace and the gift of faith remain for a far different church, if we will but have it.

Then, too, the actual church needs due appreciation. Pumped full of prejudice against the message and the life of the actual church, I have several times recently attended services, small and large, in different states, in metropolis, city, and village, and each time I have come away with a strong sense of the depth and reality of the worship and the high quality of the message. It is time theological leaders appreciated and encouraged all the good there actually is in the church. Scorn helps no one. However inadequate, I feel deeply committed to offer some constructive help to those who actually face the burdens of the concrete community, at home and abroad.

The task to realize the universal community, within trust and obedience, is by its very nature world-wide. If God's call is universal, all the world has a common need, a common standard, and a common God. In God all "foreign" lands are home; and measured by him all communities, including our actual "Christian" churches, are foreign. We all share a common God, and a common community to build under him. However wide the differences among the religions, they all share a common human nature, long and heavy accumulations of distorted doctrine, and cultural, spiritual alienation from God. This combination makes the task of transformation in "Christian nations" no easier, I believe, than in the long spaces of the non-Christian world.

The God who is universal, unconditional love needs remade men in order to effect the open, inclusive community.

He needs universal men. The Christian faith claims that in Christ God became man, and that by becoming man effected for the first time true man. Therefore Chalcedon, the creedal affirmation that in Jesus Christ were combined, without false division within him and with no merger, true God and true man, is nothing less than normative psychology. Man in process to be fulfilled became the intended product in Jesus Christ when a true human being became genuinely and fulfillingly indwelt by God.

Chalcedon thus means that man becomes man only in right relation to God. Apart from such a relation man can be neither fully man nor truly man. Man finds himself and his community only in proportion to his being rightly related to God. God remains God beyond man, without confusion, to be worshiped, trusted, and obeyed, but God also enters man's inner life, cleansing, directing, and empowering his life. Sin and failure both root in man's being out of proper relation to God, be it through faithlessness and rebellion or through lack of knowledge. Both sin and failure can be overcome only by accepting the twofold right relation to God in terms of the forgiveness that heals from beyond man and the Spirit that helps from within him. Light, forgiveness, and power for newness of life came conclusively in the kind of life Jesus lived and taught, the life he was by virtue of his fulfilling Sonship to God.

The Christian faith thus offers man ultimate help through right relation to God, through the forgiveness of his sin, through trust and through the kind of love for which he is made. Thus the Christian faith is also normative psychology. Christian missions is basically men finding their true selves as well as their true community.

When men appropriate such relation to God in such community and such life they will find the creative concern that unconditionally sets out to transform all life with a new vision and a new power. The faith comes first; the implications and implementations of such faith are as inevitable as its acceptance. "By their fruits ye shall know them." Thus Christian mission intrinsically encompasses all of life and holds inexhaustless implications for every civilization.

A theology of missions adds nothing to the Christian faith. It simply *is* the faith through and through. The universal God has given us the prescription within a living freedom to work it out, for the universal community and the universal man. The Christian community in its essential nature is normative sociology and normative psychology, forever both reliably prescriptive and boundlessly open for creative living. I believe that the Christian faith is final for men, but that its very finality is a constant call to creative adventure of both faith and life.

7: Reflections on the Basis of the World Council of Churches

Ever since the announcement of the proposed basis of the World Council of Churches in its original short form, "Jesus Christ as God and Savior," I have been deeply dissatisfied with it and have wanted it changed. As a matter of fact, long before the World Council was officially formed I wanted to propose a formula of a different nature: "Jesus Christ, Son of God, Son of Man, Savior." Or "The World Council is composed of churches who in faith and order, life and work accept Jesus Christ as Son of God, Son of Man, Savior."

When the Utrecht formula was ratified at Amsterdam, using as its basis only the phrase "Jesus Christ as God and Savior," I was deeply pained by what to me was its frightful inadequacy. I refrained from doing anything about it, however, because I understood that the basis itself was not subject to discussion. This kind of one-sided Christological statement was necessary, we were told, in order to induce some of the conservative Orthodox and Catholic groups to join—groups that were as a matter of fact deathly afraid of liberalism in the church, particularly of the American variety. As an agreement of a most delicate political nature, I had been advised that the basis was not subject to change but was more like a permanent constitution on which the World Council of Churches was founded.

But years later at St. Andrews the proposal was made and subsequently accepted at New Delhi that "according to the Scriptures" be added to the basis. New Delhi also added the trinitarian formula. Many drives went into this extension of the creed besides the demand of the Russian Orthodox Church.

On the whole, however, I believe that the change has made the situation worse rather than better. The basis, I still believe, is even more in need of change. One of the secretaries of the World Council years ago spent a long time with me, almost in tears over the heretical nature of the basis. I believe that his objections would still be the same, only with added intensity. Mine are.

What, then, are my objections? Not only as a theologian, but also as a charter member of the Faith and Order Commission to deal with Christology, I am not only especially concerned but have had the benefit of rather unusually informed discussion of the issues over a period of years. My objections are twofold: first, the basis is severely heretical from the point of view of the Christian faith; second, it is such a self-protective and self-promoting statement of an in-group that it stands in the way of effective relations to other religions and to the world in general. If the basis were both Christian and true, then I should not mind either its offensiveness or its poverty as a means of communicating and relating the faith. As it is, however, its greatest offense comes from the heretical nature of the confession.

First, then, the statement is heretical in the sense that it is true neither to the full, central New Testament picture of Christ nor to its historical development by the fathers of the church. Perhaps even these formulations need to be clarified and reinterpreted in terms of the deepest reality and meaning of Christ as he underlies the biblical and the historical interpretation, but at least we should not further falsify the true gospel message.

The statement of the World Council, "Jesus as God," is sheer Docetism. It makes no mention of Jesus' humanity. Jesus is not God but the Son of God. Most of the Christian tradition has been gracious and humble enough to admit at least this much of the truth of Incarnation. Jesus Christ is God Incarnate, not God in himself.

But God Incarnate is only one side of Jesus Christ. Jesus was also man, true man in general and real man in particular. In him God's fullness dwelt: hence his deity. But Jesus Christ is Son of Man in the sense of full humanity as well as Son of God in the sense of authentic Godhood. Neither aspect must be minimized in the true understanding of the Incarnate Word.

There is a decisive difference between the affirmation that Jesus Christ is God and Savior and that God was in Christ reconciling the world to himself. In Japan I had a long train ride with E. Stanley Jones, who kept complaining that while the Bible says "the Word became flesh" the theologians dare say no more than "the Word became the Word." The distinction between the two kinds of affirmations involves the whole meaning of God's purpose in creation and of the consequent work of Christ in redemption. Unless the eternal Word took human form fulfillingly in a real personality like us, winning the victory in and with man from within man's common, concrete situation, the Incarnation is neither real nor relevant. It is then a compensating myth to ease man's bitter lot, not a historic fact to change man's life and destiny. The Incarnation is God's purpose from the beginning, to win for, in, and with man—yes, to win within man's freedom, to win without violation of human personality, to win in a natural, fulfilling relation the full, consummating victory over sin, law, and death.

Therefore to separate Jesus from man instead of uniting him with man is to belittle, indeed destructively to curtail the Incarnation. To remove Jesus as a man from all experience of sin, repentance, and glorious victory is to miss the main point of God's purpose in creation. For the victory won consummatingly over all man's enemies is not even so much in human history—though truly a breakthrough there —as in God's eternal purpose. God created man for himself by making him a true self in process and product, and he did this by means of first estrangement from God and then the consequent willing acceptance of his love.

The distance between God and man became so deep and profound that it had to be bridged by God, from God's side, but by means of a bridge that nevertheless required man's walking over it. Man must willingly and freely come to God.

Therefore "God became human to make us divine," to share and make possible the right relation to himself within which alone we can become truly and fully human. The basis of the World Council, definitely Docetic as it is—at least by omission—therefore fails to convey the very central meaning and nature of the Incarnation.

To add "according to the Scriptures" may help somewhat because there is a strong early strand in the New Testament, especially in the Acts of the Apostles, as to the real manhood of Jesus. That Jesus was "a man anointed by God" is one of the several Christologies of the New Testament. Therefore the addition of the biblical foundation can implicitly amend what is lacking in the basis of the World Council. But since no intention to this effect has been stated the likely result, on the contrary, is a general assumption that the heretical basis is actually Scriptural. Besides, the formula shifts the weight from Christ himself, God as universal Love Incarnate, as authority over Scripture to an indiscriminate biblicism.

There is very little, as a matter of fact, in the New Testament about Jesus being God. According to most strands he is Messiah or Son of God with power. Where Jesus is called God, the expression is mostly ejaculatory or doxological, and comes at that from the less central sections of the New Testament. To magnify this strand at the even implicit expense of the other strands and to all but substitute it for the main line of historical theology leading to Chalcedon is not only a capital mistake but incalculably damaging to the Christian faith. No wonder that there is deep concern about the unbiblical and unhistorical nature of the basis of the World Council of Churches.

But I am equally concerned that the basis constitutes a

false obstacle to communication with the other religions of the world. Hendrik Kraemer has suggested that conversation among the religions of the world has only really begun. Is it not unfortunate to have to carry on such conversation from an untenable and divisive basis?

Let me illustrate my point. In Wilmette, Illinois, my wife and I visited the beautiful Baha'i Temple. There we saw all the religions depicted as under one God. Upon leaving, my wife said, "The idea is wonderful, but how unfortunate that each religion must push its own prophet. Why do the Baha'is have to insist that Ba'ull'ah is God's last revelation and normative for our age?" In Bangalore, India, I heard a theological student preaching at the theological college say, "We must preach Christ, not God. The Hindus believe in God. The Muslims believe in God. We must preach Christ. He belongs to us; Christ is our message." The whole tone was of a defensive, in-group psychology.

After speaking at the Indian Institute of World Culture in the same city on God's work in human history and winning much acceptance for the Christian view of God's purpose with and in history, even from the Hindu professor of history who presided, I received the following comment from a leading non-Christian scholar: "What divides the world of religions is not the reality or the idea of God. I think God as Universal Love most intelligent people would be able to accept from whatever religion. What divides the world of religion is the way each religion claims to know him. It is the partial loyalties that divide men in religion as elsewhere."

When Jesus is claimed to be God and men are asked to accept such a confession, they can easily be asked to become idolatrous. To substitute Jesus for God is idolatry. Such a myth will be a hindrance to countless intelligently seeking worshipers longing for a truly universal faith. When Jesus is understood as the Way, the Truth, and the Life of God's fulfilling presence and power in man, on the other hand, or as the Incarnate Love who reveals both God's nature and man's for forgiveness and fulfillment, then Jesus Christ becomes the consummating fact and symbol of God's purpose and presence in human history and of man's rightful relation to God in trust, forgiveness, and remaking. We then worship the eternal God, as he was in Christ reconciling the world unto himself.

In this way Jesus Christ becomes central both to human history and to human life, both to the biblical revelation and to human relations in general. He is God's fulfilling presence in and with man's freedom, in one of us, for all of us. Here is our hope; here is our power for reviewing and renewing human life and human history.

I submit that the World Council at least does not express this faith explicitly in its basis but rather implicitly tends to obscure and to deny it. Therefore it is not good enough even if it is considered to be an agreement rather than a confession. Perhaps men must live by myths rather than by truth, or perhaps myths become more effective truths religiously than the actual facts, whether historically or analytically. The clear truth of God's Incarnate Love may be too startling for most men.

My own conviction is that the Christian faith has had so little actual power in human history because it has not dared to accept as its central confession the full meaning and even deeper mystery that God was in Christ reconciling the world to Himself in order that we all might attain in the end, by the same victorious grace, to "true manhood, even the measure of the stature of the fullness of Christ."

8: Redefining the Task of Christian Missions

Christian missions, unless they represent universal truth, have no right to interfere in other religions and cultures. My first conviction is that both religious and sociological relativisms are severely limited categories. We proclaim the Christian faith because it is true; it is not true merely because it is Christian. The Christian faith, I believe, is man's final truth in regard to the ultimate nature of things, and therefore it also best fulfills man's deepest needs.

Consequently the missionary is everywhere at home. Whatever truth is found everywhere and anywhere belongs to the Christian. There is only one truth for man (not of man): God's living, loving will for his whole creation.

For this reason the missionary accepts eagerly all truth in every religion and culture. He accepts what is common among and within religions. Islam worships God through an interpretation quite akin to Calvinism; we join at least in worshiping the one God. Hinduism in large measure worships God and maintains the integrity of righteousness and freedom. Buddhism proclaims that ultimate religious reality is not of this world, that we must find the permanent reality beyond suffering and change. Shinto finds religious reality in the extraordinary working through the natural. In all these points we join.

The task, then, is to inquire along with others into the fullest possible universal. Here we shall meet many problems stemming both from those who believe that a personal God is not universal enough and from those who worship smaller gods. From experience of honest, undefensive discussion with exponents of other religions, I have learned that the way is wide open to Christian witness if we have the creative competence to suggest and sustain more universal categories.

A universal approach involves a universal interpretation of Jesus Christ. Most Christian theology, West and East, is a defensive, in-group rationalization built around the uniqueness of Jesus Christ. But if Jesus Christ is unique he is not universal. The unique has no relevance for the general. Jesus Christ is not unique but final, because he is the universal relation between God and man.

Jesus Christ is neither only God nor only man, but the incarnate God, the Word made flesh, not only historically in Jesus in a pioneering and perfecting way, but potentially for all men. Nothing can more disastrously defeat the Christian missionary enterprise than to declare that Jesus was God in contradistinction to all men. Such a claim is both false and divisive.

In Jesus' life, teaching, death, and resurrection we both meet God who has come to us in him and discover the universal nature of man. Man is truly man only when he is in right relation to God. Christ is perfect God-man, historically and conclusively in Jesus. As such he is historically unique, but Christ is also realized in others preparatorily before and consummatorily after Jesus and is to be realized in all men according to God's eternal purpose in God's eternal reaches of time.

Christ is God's Incarnate Word throughout the whole length and breadth of creation and human history, focused decisively in Jesus, but centered ever and always in God himself. The Holy Spirit, the reality of God's eternal relation, could be given only when the historic Jesus was taken away from the disciples.

Christ is God's universal love for men in creation and human history, as men come to know and accept him whose nature is seen actually and symbolically in Jesus as the Christ. Jesus Christ is a historic combination, a needful focus for worship and thought. He is not the eternal God, the Father. We worship the God who came in Jesus: the Christ, the Incarnate Word, available to all.

The Christian missionary must perceive the universal nature of the gospel even though to do so means a courageous rethinking and reformulation of two thousand years of Christian theology. If this is done competently, the Christian missionary can proclaim a universal gospel and be at one with all truth within any religion, except as the religion in content and practice denies the universal love of the living God.

More and more I believe in a completely Christ-centered gospel, the message of what God has done and will do through his Incarnate Word. But no gospel is Christ-centered that is not by that very fact entirely God-centered. History centers in eternity. But since God is the Creator who glories in productive variety, the universal gospel means not sameness but difference of approach. Therefore a Christ-centered theology varies with each country and region. Theology as man's response is always culture-conditioned. Hence theology, as well as worship and Christian mores, must differ from place to place and take on the natural coloration of its properly distinctive background.

We need to resolve the conflicting chords of Western Christianity into a symphony of Christian life and thought. Christianity becomes universal only as the voices of all varied backgrounds, expressed through every creative form, join in a pluralistic rendering of God's faithful love in Christ. Let all regions of the world from within their own distinctive religious, social, political, and artistic backgrounds body forth a Christian theology so rich, varied, and free that it can fulfill the deepest cravings of all peoples and glorify God in manners so diverse that they cannot help but fascinate and stimulate those of different backgrounds.

Education is a central, natural avenue for the spreading of the Christian faith. Most non-Christian countries have high respect for education and a strong craving for it. Christian education is indirect evangelization. Less and less I believe in "evangelistic services" and more and more in evangelism. Evangelism is witness for decision. But evangelism without education easily lends itself to mere proselytizing, which is more a change of name than of nature and purpose through a new and fuller relation to God.

Christian education needs to be rooted in Christian theology. Such education is the preparation for evangelism, and to have integrity it must be for its largest part on the level of creation. But God's total way can never be understood apart from a knowledge of his indirect working in nature and history. Most secularization of the modern world has come through education. To give depth to the meaning of life and to lend direction and dynamic to knowledge we need a Christian context of education. Christian theology is never revealed but is the outworking of the facts discovered by objective inquiry within the context of the universal concern and integrity that are central to the Christian's trust in God.

Modern man's religion, the way he looks at the nature of things, is formed mostly by his education. His faith is shaped by what he accepts as knowledge. Actually all education presupposes contexts that cannot be proved but which nonetheless shape and direct knowledge. In order to have a Christian direction of life, as formed and motivated by knowledge, Christians must be willing to contend with integrity in the market of truth. I am convinced that this market is open and that the Christian faith has immeasurable treasures to offer from mines which as yet have not only not been worked but not even properly located.

An institution that impressed me far beyond even good expectations was the International Christian University in

Tokyo. In addition to combining in a peculiar manner good scholarship with Christian education and vision, it works to make knowledge a matter of personal appropriation and critical understanding. Most education outside the United States is too rigidly bound to a prescribed syllabus of knowledge, with honors consisting in an external mastering of information. International Christian University has done remarkable service to the whole East by its pioneering insistence on personal understanding and evaluation of knowledge. In championing critical judgment as well as creative reason, I.C.U. is only expressing the fullness of the Christian faith in its bearing on education.

If the Christian faith is to master modern knowledge enough to deliver its institutions from secularized fashions and fashionings of knowledge, we must have, I believe, ecumenical Christian universities where potential teachers for our Christian institutions in general can be trained by creative scholars who teach all subjects from within Christian presuppositions. What a task, all the way from astronomy and geology all through the natural sciences to the social sciences and the humanities as a whole! The task seems insurmountable, but it can be mastered. I believe that four to six such ecumenical universities would be sufficient. We could make a start in Asia with such natural potentials as International Christian University in Japan and Serampore University in India.

The Christian faith cannot be less than fully committed to Christian higher education in today's crucial decisions as to the ultimate meaning and way of life. Christian education must be linked in constant, creative communication with secular and non-Christian education in a spirit of common concern for truth and for life.

The third area of constructive missionary enterprise is Christian service. In this area the church has contributed immeasurably to the non-Christian world. It has pioneered the education of women. I have a personally vivid impression of such services in Japan and the Middle East. The church has started and furthered first-class medical services.

My own acquaintance with examples of these is in Burma and in India. Missions to lepers and the physically handicapped, and other reaches of the faith only augment the work of the many first-class hospitals. To see them in action is to appreciate with deep thankfulness the services of the church. What of developments of the languages themselves, translations of religious literature as well as of the Bible, what of agricultural and technological improvements, and what of relief work, the sheer feeding and sheltering of refugees, the hungry, the unfortunate of every kind?

To minimize the practical services is to shortchange our faith. Some are now inclined to dismiss such help as "American activism," a substitute for the gospel, the soothing of our sore consciences. It is nothing of the kind. It is Christianity in action.

Some complain that to help people physically without changing their faith is to make it easier for them to hold onto the inadequate faith that is the root cause of their physical lacks. Others say that we ought never to give anything except in Christ's name—in other words, we should help people only on the condition of, or at least for the sake of, their becoming Christian.

Any such stipulation denies the Christian faith itself at its heart. We reach out to help all human need simply because it is there and we have concern for it. We are, to be sure, centrally concerned with the people's relation to God, with their salvation as total beings; but regardless of their response to God or to our faith, we love them and help them in all respects for themselves. "A cup of cold water" given in Christ's name does not mean primarily for the sake of their changing their faith, but in the spirit of Christ who loved and helped all for no ulterior motive.

Services can be a means to proselytizing mostly as the promotion of an institution, or they can be the community acting out its genuine concern for the people. When we live our faith, it is true that being and acting are ways of authentic witnessing and of winning in the dimension of Christian depth beyond all mere changing of labels. I am convinced that the Christian church will never suffer loss from being genuine in its motivation.

But some say that the state is now taking over such services all over the world, and our services are no longer needed. The answer is that as yet the need is unlimited. If the times comes when the state does take over adequately all needed human services in these fields, as well as at home, it will be up to us to prove that the faith will not dry up under such circumstances, as it seems to have done in Sweden.

Working with the state for human welfare, the church has its own distinctive area of contribution—man's total relation to God and, under him, with each other. We must stand ready to face the possibility of such a new age with a new way of relating ourselves to our total task. But as yet such a situation is mostly theoretical and should in no way discourage our attempt at sheer human helpfulness, which is desperately needed in practically all areas of the world.

Our abiding task is to proclaim God's universal love in Christ in such a winning way that there shall be no false obstacles but every true inducement to its acceptance. Our task all over the world is to live our trust in God for all men, a trust that generates concern for education and services. The fundamental demand upon us is for a theology of missions that will completely convince us that the kind of life Christ is and the kind of community his life and teaching made possible—the open, creative, inclusive community of concern through faith in the living God—are the only way to salvation, now and in the life to come.